BILLIE
PIPER

BILLIE PIPER

THE ROLLERCOASTER LIFE OF BRITAIN'S HOTTEST STAR

CHRIS STEVENS

Michael O'Mara Books Limited

First published in 2006 by
Michael O'Mara Books Limited
9 Lion Yard
Tremadoc Road
London SW4 7NQ

A CIP catalogue record for this book is available from the
British Library.

This book has not been approved, licensed or endorsed by
Billie Piper.

ISBN (10 digit): 1-84317-222-4
ISBN (13 digit): 978-1-84317-222-2

3 5 7 9 10 8 6 4 2

Designed and typeset by E-Type
Plate section designed by Button Group plc

Printed and bound in Great Britain by Cox & Wyman,
Reading, Berks

www.mombooks.com

CONTENTS

AUTHOR'S ACKNOWLEDGEMENTS

Many thanks to everybody who helped to make this biography a pleasure to research and to write. Special thanks to Matthew Sweet, for being so generous with his insights, his anecdotes and his mobile-phone bill; to my colleague David Smith of *The Observer*, for opening his contacts book; to Lindsay Davies and Kate Gribble, my editors; to Heather Holden-Brown, for making it all possible; and to James Pryor at hhb, who has an unerring instinct for the best tea rooms.

Thanks are also due to the music journalists and BBC insiders who would prefer not to be named, but who have given me invaluable help all the way through this project. I am also indebted to the many journalists whose questions have drawn such a fascinating range of responses from Billie, her family, her friends and her colleagues throughout her career. During my research for this book I was surrounded by more than 8,000 interviews and articles from magazines and newspapers, comprising about 1.5 million words of background. Wherever I have used a quote by or about Billie that sheds extra light on her character and her emotions, I have tried to credit both the interviewer and the publication.

Extra special thanks to Nicky, for her unlimited patience. I couldn't have done this, or anything else, without you.

Chris Stevens, June 2006

PICTURE ACKNOWLEDGEMENTS

Page 1: Camera Press Digital

Page 2: Ilpo Musto / Rex Features (above); Sutton-Hibbert / Rex Features (below)

Page 3: Nick Tangley / AAD / Empics (above); Tony Kyriacou / Rex Features (below)

Page 4: Brian Rasic / Rex Features (above); © Doug Peters / allaction.co.uk / Empics (below)

Page 5: Photo News Service / Rex Features

Page 6: © Jeff Spicer / Alpha (left); © Mark Allan / Alpha (right)

Page 7: Getty Images

Page 8: Getty Images

Page 9: Richard Young / Rex Features

Page 10: Richard Young / Rex Features (left); Getty Images (right)

Page 11: Jonathan Furniss / AAD / Empics (above); Getty Images (below)

Page 12: Humphrey Nemar / www.expresspictures.com (above); Dennis Stone / Rex Features (below)

Page 13: Stefan Rousseau / PA / Empics (above); Rex Features (below)

Page 14: © James Aylott / Mike Carillo / allaction.co.uk / Empics

Page 15: Steve Bell / Rex Features (above); Getty Images (below)

Page 16: Glenn Harvey / Rex Features (above); INS News Group / www.expresspictures.com (below)

Page 17: © Sean McMenomy / Corbis Outline

Page 18: © Universal / Everett / Rex Features (above); Alpha (centre & below)

Page 19: Huw John / Rex Features (above); bigpicturesphoto.com (below)

Page 20: bigpicturesphoto.com

Page 21: David Fisher / Rex Features (left); Richard Young / Rex Features (right)

Page 22: Huw John / Rex Features

Page 23: © Lee Jenkins / Corbis Outline (above); Jon Furniss / Wireimage.com (below)

Page 24: Yui Mok / PA / Empics (above); bigpicturesphoto.com (below)

1 SHE'S A STAR

Rose Tyler is facing the most crucial decision of her life. Her boyfriend is hugging her knees, begging her to stay with him. And a mysterious stranger in the doorway of a blue police box is inviting her to join him. 'It goes anywhere in the universe,' he says, 'free of charge.'

Her boyfriend hugs her harder. Rose mumbles that she has to go and find her mum.

'OK,' says the stranger. 'See you around.'

The box disappears with an echoing screech.

And then it comes back.

The stranger reappears in the doorway.

'By the way,' he says. 'Did I mention it also travels in time?'

Billie Piper was fifteen years and nine months old. She was living at her parents' home in Swindon. She was studying for her GCSEs, and she'd been seeing a boy called David for ages. And now it was a Sunday afternoon and she was sitting beside the phone, trying to take in what she had just heard.

'I sort of freaked out,' she said a few days later to *The Independent*. 'I didn't move for a little while. I just tried to sit there and take it in. But I couldn't, so I got up and started screaming.'

The call had come from her record company, Innocent – a name that reflected the age range of their target market, pre-teen girls. Billie's first single, 'Because We Want To', had been out for seven days and had sold more than 80,000 copies.

The news was incredible: 'Because We Want To' had entered the charts at number one. She was the youngest pop star ever to achieve that, and the youngest female singer to top the British singles chart since Helen Shapiro in 1961.

This was what she'd dreamed of all her short life. Since she was four years old, Billie had been dressing up and dancing in front of the TV, singing along to *Top of the Pops* with a mop or a broom handle for a microphone.

When the first flush of screaming excitement had passed, she ran to find her parents. 'I told my dad, and he said, "You'll always be number one in my eyes." That's my dad.'

The family celebrated, and there was a live interview with Radio 1's Mark Goodier, but by 9.45 that evening Billie was tucked up in bed, after toasting her triumph with a cup of tea. She had to be up before dawn the next day, to appear on Channel 4's *The Big Breakfast*.

That Sunday was 5 July 1998, the first pinnacle in a rollercoaster ride that would hurtle her through a succession of hit singles, a tabloid furore about her party-loving lifestyle, a traumatic love affair with another pop star, death threats, public collapses and a front-page burnout, a whirlwind romance and marriage to a multi-millionaire media mogul almost twice her age, estrangement from her parents, a two-year retreat from stardom, the rebirth of her career on TV, marital breakdown, and national acclaim as an actress in one of Britain's best-loved shows, *Doctor Who*.

Even though her first record made her an overnight sensation, success had not come easily or instantly. She'd been working towards it for years. 'Billie's been prepared for fame,' the managing director of Innocent, Hugh Goldsmith, told *The Times*. 'It's what she's wanted since she was ... nothing. She's been in *Evita* and *EastEnders*. She's not new to the media and entertainment industry.'

What Goldsmith could have added was that a star like Billie had existed in his imagination before he even saw her in an ad campaign for the teen magazine *Smash Hits*. He had launched the boy band Take That and crooners Robson and Jerome, and had seen the Spice Girls storm the charts with a series of platinum singles, opening the market to a younger generation of pop fans – children as young as seven or eight.

In late 1997, as the Innocent label was launched by Virgin Records, Goldsmith told John Pavely, his head of marketing, that he had a hunch that fans would adore a sassy, teenage pop singer who could dance like Madonna ... if they could find one.

'Literally within three or four days of having that conversation, Billie popped up in front of me on the cover of *Music Week*, in an ad for *Smash Hits*. I thought, "Blimey, she looks fantastic. God knows if she can sing, but I've got to meet her."'

He contacted her parents and her London theatre school to arrange a meeting and then a studio session, where she performed a demo of an R. Kelly song, 'G.H.E.T.T.O.U.T.' Billie, Goldsmith discovered, could dance and act as well as possessing a powerful, soulful voice. And Madonna was her hero.

'She looked like the girl next door – but better,' Pavely told *Red* magazine. 'She looked like you could be her friend … someone you could talk to if you wanted.'

Innocent hired a songwriting team, Wendy Page and Jim Marr, and booked time in a studio to find out what Billie could do with a pop tune. The results were so good that several of the tracks appeared on her debut album, *Honey To The B*, nine months later. Pavely declared himself 'gobsmacked'.

Goldsmith was also knocked out. As he later told *The Independent on Sunday*: 'I was instantly taken with her. She had that indefinable quality you look for in a star. A combination of a very strong look, very strong features. Almost like a beautiful manga cartoon character. Huge smile, utterly charming, just a delightful girl.'

But he knew the risk he was taking. Billie had won a scholarship to the Sylvia Young Theatre School in north London at twelve, she was a veteran of stage shows and TV sets as an extra, and her talent was unmissable. But she was still just fifteen, six years away from the age when many young people get their first job. And he was about to commit a fortune to promoting his label's first star. If it turned out to be a mistake, it might be the last one of his own career.

Innocent refused to say exactly how much they spent to make 'Because We Want To' a chart-topper: 'Whatever we deem collectively necessary,' sniffed a spokesman. But Goldsmith admitted to *The Independent* at the time, 'It doesn't come cheap. In today's climate, you are looking at a £1-million investment to launch a pop act.'

To win a new audience, new tactics were called for. Billie quit school in April – though her studies continued, with a private tutor, by legal requirement – and embarked on a British tour ... of primary schools. Talking to the *Evening News* in Scotland as she prepared for her first performance in a school gym, she explained she had already appeared at a Radio 1 road-show, performed at under-eighteen discos and done an MTV gig for eight-year-olds at the Hammersmith Odeon, alongside boy band Five.

'This is the very first time I have ever appeared at a primary school,' she told reporters. 'They will be a lot younger than I am used to, but having got together my own little show with four songs and lots of competitions, I hope it will go well.'

That was at Bruntsfield Primary in Montpelier, Edinburgh, with another show to follow in the afternoon at South Morningside Primary. Subsequent dates were booked across Britain, in cities from London to Aberdeen, with flying visits to Europe, including an appearance in Sweden. All of this was build-up: 'Because We Want To' would not be released until the end of June.

It was the pre-teen equivalent of the indie college circuit, except many of these shows started at 8.50 a.m. in assembly. The gigs followed a pattern – costume changes in the girls' toilets, a rubber-ball entrance as Billie bounced on to the stage, and lots of shouting: 'Hi everyone! Any birthdays out there? Cool!' And then the whole school would be bopping and chanting, 'Because we want to! Because we want to!'

By early May she was already feeling the strain. 'I feel like my feet haven't touched the ground,' she told the *Sunday Mirror*. 'I've been doing hundreds of interviews and shooting videos, and I haven't got a day off till August. God knows how the Spice Girls have managed to keep it going for so long.'

'You have to work so hard at this,' she added to the *Evening News*, 'and when you have your schooling and stuff on top of that, it can get a bit much. I have to do ten hours of school work a week, which is tough, although it has been explained this is the busiest part of my musical career with the all-important first single coming out.'

Comments like that revealed a side to her character which Innocent hadn't bargained for, one that would challenge everyone who tried to keep a lid on Billie Piper for years to come: she liked to talk. And she didn't hide her feelings. Ask her a question, and the answer came from the heart.

Innocent reacted by appointing two full-time press officers to chaperone her through every interview, and rehearsing her responses. Questions about money, for instance, got a stock answer: 'I can't be bothered with all

that stuff.' If Blanche Hague, one of the guardians, suspected a newspaper photographer was trying to get a
revealing shot by looming over her charge, she would
hiss: 'Billie! Cleavage!' This was rock 'n' roll with
Victorian values.

The piece of luck Innocent needed to guarantee a
perfect launch came from something far outside their
control. The day after 'Because We Want To' finally
went on sale, England played Argentina in the World
Cup. David Beckham was sent off for flicking a kick at
Diego Simeone after a foul, and a ten-man England
team was dumped out of the competition on penalties.

The nation was outraged. Beckham's effigy was
lynched outside a London pub, and one tabloid printed
a dartboard with his face over the centre. More importantly for Billie, sales of the current number one – the
football anthem 'Three Lions' by Baddiel, Skinner and
the Lightning Seeds – dropped dead. The song that had
topped the charts for three weeks was suddenly a tune
no one wanted to hear.

Instead of that terraces chant, the new tune lodging
like fish-hooks in every pop fan's brain was raucous,
staccato and funny. Billie opened the chorus in a
querulous, matronly tone, and back came the response,
cheeky and brash, from Billie herself and a team of
singers even younger, all shouting out the title of the
song at the very tops of their voices: 'Because we want
to! Because we want to!' *The Independent* called it, 'A
good pop song … its lyrics raise it to the level of a veri-
table anthem of teen power.'

'It's a young person's comment,' Billie admitted to *The Sun*. 'I can imagine millions of mums and dads cursing me because their kids will be saying it all the time. I represent Youth Power, and I hope being number one helps inspire young people to do what they want. "Because We Want To" is about being youthful and rebellious in a positive way.'

If she thought she had been busy before, the pace was now breakneck. Due to embark on a European tour within days of hitting number one, Billie was suddenly doing a dozen or more interviews every day, and to every reporter she said the same thing: she couldn't quite believe what was happening.

'I've always wanted to be famous, and I've been working towards this ever since I was a kid. But I'm too tired to take it all in. It still seems weird to be number one. I can't accept it at the moment. I have little outbursts and start jumping around from time to time, acting stupid. I can't even imagine or visualize how many people have bought my single. I would have been happy with a Top Ten spot, but being number one is just amazing.

'I knocked "Three Lions" off the top, which is scary. If England had won, I wouldn't be there. Some good has come out of them losing – for me, at least! I always knew I was going to be famous. I just didn't think it would happen to me so young. Two weeks ago, nobody knew who I was, but now half the population do. That's what I can't get my head round.

'I've achieved my main ambition but my hopes for

the future are that people enjoy me and my music, and that my records are successful. Now I really want to tour the world. I want to be an inspiration to other young people who want to do things like this. A lot of people have sent me emails saying, "You've inspired us to form a band," and I feel quite proud that I've given some people the will power just to do stuff.'

There was one problem, though: Billie was at a loss as to what she should splash out on with her new-found fortune. She pledged to buy her parents a generous present; the more standard pop star splurges of expensive bubbly, flash pads and fast cars being somewhat out of reach for someone so young.

The single was accompanied by a video, shot in Greenwich, south London, and broadcast almost hourly by MTV. It featured Billie as an alien beamed down to a street of terraced houses to teach the neighbourhood children her dance routine. After the Spice Girls, here was a Space Girl.

The image was wholesome – all wide eyes and cheeky grins. 'I'm too young for sex and drugs and rock 'n' roll,' she told *The Sun*'s Bizarre column. 'I think going out to showbiz parties all the time and getting drunk is a bit naff.'

Not everyone wanted to see it that way. By the end of the week, *The Guardian* had launched an attack on the trend for school-age pop stars. 'It's downright indecent, watching them comport themselves like adults before they've had much chance to be kids,' complained writer Caroline Sullivan. She cited the desperate personal problems of former child stars Lena Zavaroni and Michael Jackson, said that country music star LeAnn Rimes 'is fifteen but sounds like a thirty-year-old divorcee', and accused music-industry executives of pandering to perverts: 'Young is the way the music biz likes 'em, because it reaps both short- and long-term gains. There's the initial flurry of paedophiliac attention, which is followed, hopefully, by a profitable adult career.'

But Billie made it clear to Sullivan that she was no pushover. 'I'm not growing up too quickly. I think this job actually prepares you for life. It can be hard, this business, because people promise you things that don't happen, and it's made me grow up a lot. But I think I needed to.'

The first paparazzi photo appeared just three days after the single hit number one. Snatched at a celebration party, it showed Billie with a glass of champagne and wearing a low-cut frock, and the *Daily Mail* captioned it, 'Out on the town in a revealing slip dress.'

'I was a bit upset about that,' Billie told *The Independent*'s Tim Hulse. 'I was actually wearing a dress. There's a bit of a difference between a slip and a dress. And it wasn't revealing at all, it was just a normal dress and in fact it came down below my knees. I had about two glasses of champagne because I was celebrating my number-one record.'

She was also nettled by the *Mail*'s comment that she'd 'had a steady boyfriend for eight months'.

'That was really weird,' Billie said. 'I don't think it's relevant whether I have been going out with him for a long time or not, because I think so many girls do go out with boys for a long time now. Not that I'm saying I'm sleeping with him or anything.'

That was the first time the press had stuck its long nose around her bedroom door, though Billie could not know that they were there for keeps – and that frequently in the future they would come barging in, sometimes literally.

During that first week of fame, the intrusions and meanness came as a shock. 'It's a bit scary,' Billie told Hulse. 'I just have to be careful what I'm doing. I don't really think I'm an immature fifteen-year-old. I sort of know what I want out of life, and I know what's stupid and what's sensible. I know the pitfalls. Sometimes journalists can be a bit patronizing and manipulative, basically because I'm fifteen and they think it's all right to do that. Some journalists just pressure me. It can be quite hard sometimes. They seem to want really personal things and I do get a bit scared sometimes. They want to know things about my private life that have nothing to do with my pop career – about boys and stuff. I just think it's so irrelevant.'

The PR chaperones acted quickly to stamp out the idea that Billie had a steady boyfriend. 'Billie doesn't have any time for romance in her life right now. She's so busy with her career she hardly has a minute to herself,' a 'source' said.

Billie played along. At first she cheerfully agreed she had a boyfriend, David Price, and that he was two years older than her at seventeen. She said to *The Sun*: 'We get on really well. I like older men … not too old, though! I don't know what's going to happen between us because I'm so busy. I don't see him a lot.'

By the time her single had been number one for a week, the party line had changed: 'We had a sort of thing going, but we're just best friends now.'

The truth was messier than that, but it would not emerge until the press tired of patting and pawing at her like cats with a ball of wool. The claws would come out soon enough. And when they did, no one seemed to care if Billie was ripped apart.

2 BLIND AMBITION

When Hugh Goldsmith said Billie had been getting ready for fame ever since she was born, he was barely exaggerating. She had been working at it since she was old enough to dance, and there has never been a time when she doubted her ability to make her dreams become real.

'I have wanted to be famous for as long as I can remember,' she told *The Sunday Times* as she shot her first video. 'I started out doing drama, dance and singing locally in Swindon, and taking modelling courses in the holidays.'

Billie was born at Princess Margaret Hospital in Swindon, on 22 September 1982, on the cusp of Virgo and Libra. As a teenager, she felt Virgo didn't really suit her: 'Virgos are typically pure, innocent and cute, but I'm not a sweet girl. I'm friendly and cuddly, but I'm not a child.'

Her first step into the limelight came before she could even walk. Her parents, Mandy and Paul, had named her Leian (pronounced Lee-Ann) Paul (after her dad) Piper. But that didn't quite seem to fit their cheeky, happy baby. 'My dad went to America and heard the name Billie, came back and said I didn't look like a Leian.'

Mandy, a housewife, and Paul, a builder, went back to the register office when Billie was seven months old to notify officials of the change, and discovered a problem: the clerk, confused by Paul's decision to give his daughter his own name, had entered her gender as male. According to the forms, she was a boy.

If the muddle hadn't been spotted, the youngest girl ever to go straight to number one would have been a boy called Leian.

Billie's grandparents thought it was hilarious, and called her Bobbie. Billie, as she grew up, was less sure, as she revealed to reporters: 'When Dad called me Billie, I don't think he thought about the conse-quences at school. People really ripped it out of me. There used to be a song we sang in assembly that mentioned a billy goat, and everyone would look at me every time we sang it. So when I knew we were going to sing that song, I wouldn't go to assembly. But Dad was like, "You'll love it when you're older." And I do. People know me because of my name.'

Mandy and Paul lived on a housing estate in west Swindon, Wiltshire. Billie was an only child until she was seven, when brother Charlie arrived. Sisters Harley and Ellie followed at two-year intervals, and the family moved to a five-bedroom house. It was already clear by then that Billie's drive to perform was unstoppable, and her parents decided they had to support her ambitions.

'Billie's always loved dressing up and being the centre of attention,' Mandy told reporters, in a quote that was endlessly recycled – the Pipers rarely said a word to the press. 'She would have a broom handle or mop instead of a mike as she mimed to songs.'

Performing was her earliest memory: 'Playing the double bass with my dad when I was about four. I only sat on his shoulders; I didn't actually play. I just remember really admiring him and looking at him as if he was an angel.'

She was a theatrical child in every way. 'I wasn't a brat,' she insisted to a pop magazine. 'I was just dramatic – an emotional child. The first day I went to primary school, I didn't want to leave my mum so I kicked my teacher a few times. My sister did that too. It must be a family trait.'

At six she joined the local Sixth Sense theatre company; at nine she registered with Swindon's Tanwood dance school and casting agency. 'I was so passionate about it from a stupidly young age. Neither of my parents were at all theatrical, so I've never really understood where I got it from, but I always knew that was definitely what I wanted.

'Every Saturday morning I'd dedicate three hours to dancing in my living room to Madonna's greatest hits.' She took it so seriously she would even wear a fake mole on her upper lip. 'I don't know where I got my drive from. A lot of young people dream about being famous but I was very dedicated.'

Aged seven, she gave her first public performance. 'I remember having so much confidence that I asked my dance teacher if the rest of the class could watch me do a solo. I was so proud of it. So I performed "Vogue", and I even did a backflip. I'd never do that now.'

Her television work began at this age too, first with an American TV ad for a soft drink, Kool-Aid, and then for a breakfast cereal, 'For something like Honey Cheerios. I was only about six or seven, so it was just cool to be doing it.' She had to wear a bizarre costume, as she recalled to *The Daily Telegraph*: 'Some crazy peach leotard. I just loved it! I remember leaving London and feeling like crying. Even though it's only sixty miles up the road [from Swindon], it's a completely different way of life. And I knew that that existed and I was desperate to have it, taste it again … If there was a talent contest on, I'd be in it. My aunt and uncle used to have a camper van, and I always used to go round with them to different holiday sites and enter different shows.'

Not all the other pupils at Brook Field Primary School were impressed, and Billie suffered sneers and playground abuse. 'I hate bullying. I just want to be friends with everyone,' she said in 1999. 'But I think most people experience it at some point. With me it was more the bitchiness because I always wanted to do something which deviated from the norm.'

A few of the children laid plans to get Billie into trouble – and succeeded. 'I was called into the head's office at primary school,' she recalled. 'I'd forgotten to take my daily vitamin tablet so I took it when I got to school. My friends asked if they could have one so I gave them out. One girl said I'd given her a tablet that made her really ill. The head went mad and acted as if I was pushing drugs. It really upset me. My dad ended up phoning him and telling him off though.'

When Billie was ten, the family went on holiday to Disney World in Florida, where she met her first celebrity – E.T. The same year, she taught a group of friends some dance steps and they performed the Shangri-Las' sixties hit 'Leader Of The Pack'. She had a poster on her wall of Madonna, her role model, in the Warren Beatty movie *Dick Tracy*.

The move to Bradon Forest Secondary School in Purton, Swindon, at eleven left her feeling out of place – and those feelings grew, until she began to feel trapped. Though Billie enjoyed school and made friends easily, she wasn't academic and she didn't want to spend every day doing maths and English. Her teachers saw immediately that she was something special. She was 'the most delightful girl', said teacher Jan Taylor. 'She had a wonderfully friendly nature, was very bright and quite obviously very talented.'

The other children saw it too. Former classmate Seb Roach told reporters: 'I knew her really well. She was nice and I talked to her quite a lot. Billie always said she wanted to be a star, and she always wanted to go to acting school. All the boys fancied her.'

Though she was at Bradon Forest for less than two years, she made her impact – and the school left an impression on her. Years later, pressed for school stories by pop journalists, the memories came flooding out: 'I met my best friend Sally in secondary school. She was a lot more streetwise than me; I was a mummy's girl. She got me into trouble loads, like when I tried smoking with her and got caught. I was grounded for the whole of the summer holidays.

'I liked English and art best, but maths and science always put me on a downer. The thing is, in maths there has to be a right answer, but in English it's up to you what the right answer is. A bit like music really.'

To cheat in tests, she would hide crib notes under her skirt. 'I'd get them out and hide them under the desk. Teachers used to think I was concentrating, but I'd be reading the answers.

'I loved school dinners. I was always asking, "Is there seconds?" I loved fish fingers, Arctic rolls, and chocolate sponge with chocolate sauce. If I wanted to skive off, I used to put my head against the radiator and teachers would say, "You're off-colour – no more school for you."

'Miss Wells, my English teacher, was in charge of the school shows and always gave me good roles. And she used to really help me with my spelling.

'I was actually a bit of a tomboy at school – most of my friends were boys. My first kiss was under an acorn tree with a boy called Matthew Buckshall while he walked me home from school. I was eleven. The funny thing is we arranged it all in advance. It was a planned thing. Now when I see him I always think of him as my first kiss, and he thinks of me as his first kiss too. He's a really lovely boy. Nobody at school knew about it.'

Chocolate sponge and first kisses weren't enough to satisfy her ambitions, though. 'I think it's every little girl's dream to be famous, but when I reached about twelve, I really needed to do something to forward my career,' she said to the *Evening Post*. 'I was so ambitious, and I didn't want to stay trapped in Swindon. I wanted more. I knew that if I stayed I would end up really resenting my friends and my relationships.

'I went to my parents with a list of the reasons why I wanted to go to stage school and said, "This is what I want to do with my life." My mum and dad didn't push me into it – quite the opposite. But they were very supportive.'

Miss Wells and the drama teacher, Julia Dickinson, helped Billie attend an audition at the Sylvia Young Theatre School in Marylebone, London. Her acting ability so impressed the principal that she was awarded a half-scholarship to offset the fees, and shortly before her thirteenth birthday Billie moved to London. She lived with an aunt in Barnes, travelling home to Swindon only at weekends.

The Sylvia Young Theatre School provided the blue-print for dozens of performing arts schools or 'fame academies' across Britain. With 150 pupils aged nine to sixteen, it was once described by *The Observer* as 'a sausage factory for famous people'. Its founder doesn't disagree: 'I suppose it is, but they are individually made sausages, not mass-produced.'

From Monday to Wednesday, it is an ordinary school, with an academic curriculum that focuses on maths, science and languages. But Thursday and Friday are vocational days, and the only vocation for Sylvia's pupils is the stage. They take dance classes, acting classes, voice classes, singing classes … and since the school began in 1972 its little sausages have included Nick Berry from *Heartbeat*, Spice Girl Emma Bunton, the Appleton sisters from All Saints and TV presenter Dani Behr.

'It was much more scary than starting at a normal comprehensive school,' Billie admitted. 'I went from being the only one in the class who had that ambition, to a school where everyone wanted to do the same thing – the competition was so extreme. You're trying to make yourself known in the school, and get work and compete with the other kids, while also building friendships – that's actually quite tough. I kept my head down, so I didn't see any bitchiness. But it was hard work, and it was lonely at times, because you go from a place where you are the only person with that ambition to one where everybody is like that. It was a tough old life. But it was what you wanted, so you didn't think, "God, I am so tired, I have only had six hours' sleep." You thought, "More! More singing! More dancing! More cabaret!"'

Other pupils in her year included Matt Willis, who found fame with Busted, Lee Ryan from boy band Blue and jazz singer Amy Winehouse.

Her family wasn't forgotten. For her dad's fortieth birthday, in 1995, she put on a song-and-dance act. But the legacy of those years is a slightly awkward, distant relationship with her parents, who moved to Spain in 2002.

'I have a very weird relationship with my mother,

I think because I left home so young,' Billie told former tabloid editor Piers Morgan in an illuminating interview with *GQ* magazine in 2006. Living away from home, the young starlet experienced none of the parent–teen battles that most children frustratedly live through, only to emerge on the other side with, unexpectedly, a closer relationship with those people who have helped shape them. For Billie, her parents were people she saw at weekends: they were practically strangers, from a different generation and a different town. She didn't have to abide by their rules, she didn't *have* to listen to a word they said if she didn't want to. As she succinctly put it, 'They could hardly say, "You're grounded!" when I was living in London.'

Her parents trusted her, she believed, because they knew her obsession with acting would override any temptation to misbehave. If sometimes she felt homesick, it wasn't a big problem. 'I was a bit lonely at times, but I'm glad I did it because it paid off,' she admitted to a pop journalist. 'I was good at school, well behaved. I wasn't very academic or clever, but I couldn't be bothered to annoy or pester people, or backchat the teachers. I just wanted to do what I had to do and concentrate on my career. Occasionally I got sidetracked but on the whole I think (well, I hope) I was a good pupil. I was never naughty, but I liked watching other people mess around – it was funny!'

Theatre school was fun, but Billie was eager for the real thing. A bit-part in *EastEnders* came up, as a friend of Bianca, played by Patsy Palmer – Billie's character helped her to put on a fashion show. Then a dream came true: she got to act with Madonna. Well, almost …

'I was in *Evita* – you can see a three-second shot of my face in one scene with Jonathan Pryce. I played this young Argentinian girl, but the nearest I got to Madonna was about five yards away. I didn't actually speak to her, but just to be near her was amazing. I was nearly crying, I was so happy.'

The musical, directed by Alan Parker, was filmed at Shepperton Studios in London. Billie was fourteen and she spoke two lines.

She was a miniature Spice Girl, too, on the children's TV show *Scratchy & Co.*, performing the Girl Power hit 'Who Do You Think You Are?' Billie was Posh Spice, Victoria Adams – the future Mrs Beckham. 'It was great fun,' she said to *The Sunday Times*, 'because I adore the Spice Girls. I just sucked my cheeks in and struck a few silly modelling poses.'

Modelling was something she knew about, though at five foot five Billie was not destined for a catwalk career. Instead, her pop career was about to begin – with a piece of pink bubblegum.

Billie answered an ad in *The Stage*, the trade paper for the performing arts, and auditioned for what she thought was a one-off role in a television advert for *Smash Hits* magazine.

'*Smash Hits* saw loads of girls for that campaign,' John Pavely, marketing director at Innocent, told *The Sunday Times*. 'They all arrived at the auditions dressed to the nines. Then Billie turned up in her school uniform. I think she blew them away because she has real spark and she's naturally cool. I don't think there's anything the girl can't do. I've seen a holiday video of her when she was eight, dancing to Madonna, and even that was brilliant.'

Billie was hired for the entire summer campaign – on TV, in magazines and on advertising hoardings. For the telly ads, she ran towards the camera blowing a pink bubble and bursting out, 'Pop!'

'I had an instinct that I was going to do something good afterwards,' she said. 'It was a big job.'

Something good did happen – Innocent called. Sylvia Young had no hesitation in recommending Billie met the record executives. 'I knew Billie would be brilliant in pop,' she said. 'But she is also a fine, fine actress who can do anything from soaps to Shakespeare. It was Billie's acting ability that won her a scholarship, though she was a good dancer with a reasonable singing voice. I always expected her to become a star, but of the screen rather than pop.'

Ms Young was not shy about taking her share of the credit either. 'She's going to be huge,' she said in 1998. 'We're thrilled because it was our agency that gave her that opportunity for *Smash Hits*. When there was interest from record companies, I recommended that she sign to Innocent. It has worked out beautifully.'

The truth was that nobody – not Sylvia Young, not Paul and Mandy Piper – could have stood in Billie's way. For Billie didn't just know what she wanted: she knew what she didn't want too. She hated the small-town mentality of provincial life, and the misery it could cause: 'I saw a lot of things I didn't want to repeat,' she later told the *Radio Times* in 2006. 'Major drug abuse, living off the dole, wives beaten up by husbands. I felt very frustrated, easily bored. I wasn't starved of being a child. I was desperate to be adult, to work.'

So when the deal with Innocent arose, Billie jumped at it, going in head first and without a thought for anything but her one-way ticket to success. 'I was just determined to sign a big recording contract,' she told Piers Morgan, 'and I refused to let Dad ask too many questions. I was just like, "Sign the deal, now!" I didn't care about the small print. I remember just booting him under the table, telling him to get on with it. None of us knew what was happening. I just knew it was what I wanted.'

3 THE PRICE OF FAME

Billie turned sixteen on the eve of her second single release, and Innocent threw a party that left Billie reeling. There were three or four hundred guests; it started at eight and went on until the small hours. Billie told *The Times*: 'I got there at eight and I never sat down once.

'I was socializing all night with everyone I've worked with, and although it was nice to see everyone again I never got the chance to sit down and go, "Oh my God, this is all for me because I'm sixteen." And a year ago I would have had a party in Pizza Hut or something.'

No other sixteen-year-old would have had *The Sun*'s pop editor Dominic Mohan present her with balloons and a birthday cake at her party, either.

The new single was 'Girlfriend', a more soulful pop song than her debut hit, but one with just as catchy a chorus. The way its lyrics repeated like echoes suggested a slowed-down, loved-up version of 'Because We Want To'. It was a tested formula, and Innocent were confident.

Billie clearly understood how it worked. '"Because We Want To" was number one, so I would be disappointed if my other singles don't get there too. You have to start with a really powerful song to get into it, because that's your official stamp. A lot of people have compared it to Girl Power and the Spice Girls and all of that. That's fair enough, and I want to represent being young. There's a lot of arguments between the younger generation and the older generation because we're not given a chance to speak, or they just patronize us.

'I don't just want to be a hit in the UK,' she added. 'I want to be as famous as Madonna. I want worldwide success. I always wanted to be famous. I helped a friend who had a Saturday job in a hairdressers, and I was so bored, I hated every minute of it. I'm greedy for success. Everybody probably thinks I'm manufactured and that it's all happened overnight for me, but it really hasn't. I'm so ambitious. I want so much out of life.'

The record company intended to serve those ambitions, and America was at the top of their list. Earlier in September, Billie had flown to New York for a series of meetings with executives who would launch her US career the following spring. With press officer Blanche Hague and personal assistant Deborah Lynam escorting her through Heathrow, and a pop journalist in tow, she was clearly treating life as a big adventure. 'I'm so excited,' she kept saying. 'I've never been to New York.'

The night before, she'd slept in her parents' caravan at Rockley Park camping site in Poole, Dorset. Now she was flying in the first-class cabin of a transatlantic jumbo, and trying without success to wheedle her PA into buying her a pair of pink Nike trainers on expenses. 'Billie, it's time for your injection,' retorted Deborah, brandishing a shiny tube and, to the journalist's horror, Billie rolled up a sleeve and started slapping the crook of her arm. Then the pair of them burst into fits of giggles – the 'syringe' was a ballpoint pen, and the routine was dreamt up to tease reporters.

In Times Square, Billie posed for a photographer with a trio of NYPD cops, and bought a bag of dough-nuts, leaving her last one beside a man sleeping rough. New Yorkers appealed to her, as she explained to *Top of the Pops* magazine: 'The people here seem a lot bigger than back home. They seem to have bigger personalities. They're really friendly and excited about everything.'

Back in Swindon, she had her first experience of how thoroughly unpleasant fame can be, on an evening at the funfair with friends. A boy, no older than four-teen, peeled away from his mates and approached her. 'You're Billie,' he said. 'F**king ugly bitch.' And he slapped her.

The blow wasn't hard enough to bruise her, but she was deeply shocked. 'He only did it because he knew I couldn't hit him back,' she told friends. 'Not that I would have.'

The world was starting to lash out at her in other ways. One journalist who interviewed her several times in 1998 and 1999 remembers Billie's birthday party: 'It was a massive affair, and everybody was completely pissed. She didn't know any better and as far as I could see there was no one around her saying, "This isn't a good idea, you shouldn't be doing this." Everyone was just like, "Yeah, great, she's doing really well, we've got this star!"

'In every interview she would say how tiring she was finding it, but she would always do it in a really sweet way. It wasn't like she was sitting there moaning throughout the interview. I did really feel sorry for her at times, because some of the people around her didn't have her best interests at heart – that's the way I saw it. Some of them just rode along on her coat-tails: they went to the parties, they had a really good time. No one seemed to think that Billie was only fifteen or sixteen and shouldn't have been around the record industry's scene, going to parties and staying up late.'

Pop is a closed world. For journalists, it can be dangerous to make enemies, especially among public relations executives – talk too freely about what went on behind the scenes with one pop act, and you might find yourself barred from interviewing the next big thing. It's hard to find a pop writer with a single criticism about the teenage Billie ... but it's even harder to find one who is prepared to talk on the record, even to offer praise and positive comments.

As a result, most 'I-was-there' insights about Billie's career come from 'a source' or 'a journalist who asked not to be named'.

On Sunday 11 October, 'Girlfriend' went straight to number one. Billie was only the third artist, after Robson and Jerome and B*Witched, to achieve that double with a debut and a follow-up. One week later, her first album, *Honey To The B*, was released. Sales were slow at first, but within weeks she had sold more than half a million copies in Britain, going double platinum, with sales topping 70,000 in Japan, 50,000 in Canada and 30,000 in New Zealand.

'I haven't got a bad word to say about her,' insisted one music journalist with long experience in the industry. 'I always thought she was so lovely and such a sweet girl. She would always remember you – she was probably well trained, because a lot of these people are, and if they don't remember you they'll kind of pretend, but she was one who always knew your name and would joke with you. I always thought she was lovely, but I didn't think the people around her were terribly lovely. Some of them were great, but a couple just weren't looking after her as they should. It didn't take long for it to catch up with her, and that's when I think she started having the problems. No wonder she got exhausted, because not only was she doing the work stuff, which was really full-on, but she was partying as well.'

By the end of October, vicious rumours had started to do the rounds, fuelled by Billie's frequent appearances at pop parties. Though she was two years away from being old enough to buy a drink legally in a pub, Billie had been seen regularly with a glass of wine in her hand, while people around her were drinking hard.

It wasn't as if she was determined to live out a rock 'n' roll fantasy: she'd always wanted to be Madonna, not Janis Joplin. But there were too few people keeping an eye on her. One person who knew her said, 'I don't think Billie was the kind of brat who was really demanding, who would stamp her feet and say, "I want to do this," when people said she couldn't. I don't think anyone really thought about stopping her.'

What hit Billie hardest, though, was the final break-up of her relationship with Swindon sweetheart David Price. For months she'd been telling interviewers that she didn't have time for a boyfriend. Now her protests had come true: the four-year friendship fell apart under the strain of her schedule.

David Price was quoted in the *News of the World* two years later: 'She said she had too much work to do in her showbiz career. It took me months to get over it.'

Comments from Price had appeared in the tabloids before, when 'Because We Want To' was released. 'I didn't know whether David had gone to the press or whether one of my mates had, and they were both scary thoughts,' she admitted around Christmas 1998, after the break-up. 'That's what I have to deal with, and there's probably a lot worse to come.'

When it did come, it certainly was worse, though most of Price's descriptions of their sex life had the well-worn tone of a journalist's stock phrases and euphemisms. More believable was Price's claim about how, as teenagers, they had raided his parents' wine cellar. 'Me and Billie and my sister used to get really drunk. It was a laugh. Billie loved red wine.'

His description of seeing her *Smash Hits* ad on a bill-board also rang true: 'It really freaked me out.'

Years later, Billie used an interview in *GQ* magazine to laugh at her boastful ex, saying she had lost her virginity at fifteen with a boy she'd been seeing for three years. 'It was a bit of a disappointment the first time, obviously … It couldn't have [lasted] more than about four minutes.'

At sixteen, though, the break-up was nothing to laugh about. 'I was in love with a guy called David,' she told a reporter. 'I went out with him for about four years, on and off, and we only just recently split up and I'm still a bit upset about it. I still really like him but I'm so busy at the moment, it's not fair on him. I don't know if it was true love but he was certainly my first love. I was besotted with him and I didn't fancy anyone else. Well, actually, I did fancy other people but I didn't do anything about it.'

Run-down, miserable and suffering from stomach ache, Billie was taken into hospital for a check-up a few weeks before Christmas, and the rumour mill ground twice as hard: she was drinking too much, claimed the whispers; she was doing drugs; her record company had learned she was pregnant with Price's baby and ordered her to have an abortion.

It was that last rumour that caused Billie and her family the most anguish, and it was retold again and again over the next eighteen months, with the finger pointed at different 'fathers'. Barbs like that are almost impossible to dig out – ignore them and the whispers get louder, deny them broadly and no one believes the denial, deny them specifically and the original rumour becomes common gossip. The only other option is to sue, as another teen pop star, Jason Donovan, did in the early nineties when lies about his sexuality were widespread. Donovan won his court case, but his career was almost wiped out.

Billie's advisers decided to adopt the safest tactic, the general denial: 'The downside to all the success,' she told *The Times* carefully in December 1998, 'has been that there have been tons of untrue things said about me. It seems to happen when there isn't much other news about, that stuff gets made up and rumours start. It does get upsetting but I suppose I have to learn to take the good with the bad.'

In another interview a few days later, one of dozens over the Christmas period, she said: 'To be honest I haven't seen any drugs in this industry, even though I'm aware it goes on. When it comes to drugs I've got to be strong and just say no. I am pretty confident I won't fall into all of that drugs and partying – almost 100 per cent sure – but you can never really know what will happen. I've got a really stable family and the team that works around me is really down-to-earth. I never really think I'll get into all that stuff because that's not what I'm into. I'm aware of the pressures but it doesn't really bother me because I've always wanted to be a performer.'

She also emphasized her positive message to every reporter. 'I want to show other young people that if they work hard enough for something and want it enough then they can get it. There's more to life than hanging around smoking and drinking.

'I hope that people are intrigued by me, by my age, by how ambitious I am and how much I want to succeed.' She was well aware that other teenagers didn't necessarily have her get-up-and-go – that there were youths who were, in fact, the very opposite of her bright and bubbly self, lacking in ambition and direction and perhaps even hope. Said Billie to *The Times*: 'I just want to prove that there's more to life than just giving up. Hopefully people will look at me and say, "She's just a little girl who comes from Swindon. If she can do it, so can I."

'My family is really pleased for me, and very supportive. I don't have pushy parents. They are always anxious about whether I'm doing the right things or if I'm determined enough, but most of all they want to be sure that I'm happy.'

Eighteen months later, talking to John Dingwall of the *Scottish Daily Record*, Billie was more forthright: 'Most of what has been said is not true. I had a bad stomach infection and, apparently, that was down to me having an abortion. I couldn't understand why anyone would think that of a fifteen-year-old pop star. There wasn't any dirt to dig so it was easy to make something up and accuse me of things that weren't true.'

The intensity of the vitriol baffled Innocent's execs. Here was a talented, entertaining performer, hardworking, from a nice family, who didn't have a bad word to say about anyone. She was always upbeat, she had time for everyone and there wasn't an arrogant bone in her body. It was difficult to find anything to dislike, let alone a reason for this poisonous gossip.

'I interviewed her many times,' one journalist agreed, 'and she was just really sweet. She's a very genuine person. Perhaps that's because she started when she was so young, but even when she was only fifteen the fame didn't ever seem to go to her head. I was always struck by how down-to-earth she was. I first met her right back in the beginning when she first got her record deal. I was young at the time, but I remember thinking, "My God, you're so young – it's ridiculous." She was very sweet, really friendly, but she seemed quite worldly for her age. She had quite a lot of people around her, looking after her. Maybe it's a stage-school thing, but she never seemed to be fazed by things. Which seemed weird.'

Songwriter Wendy Page, who co-wrote both the first hit and the album's title track, tried to rationalize the pressures Billie faced to *The Times*: 'If I didn't know her, I'd probably say she's too young for the music business. But I do know her, and I think she has the talent, the ambition and the ability to be around for a very long time indeed. She also works hard and is very level-headed about it all. She's very intelligent.'

The intensity of Britain's love-and-hate affair with Billie was highlighted at the *Smash Hits* awards. *Mirror* journalist Matthew Wright had been turned away from 1997's ceremony after the Spice Girls objected to his presence. This year he had a chance for revenge, when a pre-press copy of the magazine, containing details of the prize-winners, was sent to him in error.

Broadcasting the results a week early, he revealed that Billie had scooped Best Female Solo Star, Best Dressed Female and Princess Of Pop.

She was also named Worst Female Singer and overall Sad Loser Of '98, and took prizes for Worst Single and Worst Album too. As if that wasn't bad enough, her third single, 'She Wants You', failed to make number one. Billie gritted her teeth and tried to ignore the carping voices who told her that failure was inevitable – she had started at the top so the only way was down. But to see the single stall at number three was frustrating.

The glare of the spotlight was getting more intense by the month. 'To be honest, I never imagined this,' she admitted. 'It has happened extremely fast so I'm still coming to terms with it and accepting it all. I actually quite like the thought of people seeing me grow up, although I do need my own space and time. Emotionally I'm sixteen. I mean, I still cry when my dad shouts at me.

'When you're tired all you think about are the negative things, and you're like, "Everyone hates me, nobody likes me." But it's about being emotionally strong, which takes a long time … You can learn a dance routine in a day, but you can't learn to be emotionally strong in a day. It's something that needs plenty of experience.'

Comments like that were always followed by something more upbeat, as if she was constantly trying to pull herself together. This to the *Herald and Weekly Times*: 'The way I look at it is that you only live once. You have to enjoy what you're doing, otherwise what's the point?'

On top of the interviews and the performances, she was still trying to study for her GCSEs. 'Homework is a headache,' she complained to pop paper *Melody Maker*. 'I know I don't want to be an accountant. I will always want to be a performer. I don't need equations and algebra to help me perform on stage. Percentages are good if you're going to a sale, though.'

It's a protest that any sixteen-year-old could make, but in Billie's case it was true.

To make it worse, she was now living out of hotels. 'I find some things can get a bit tedious and tiring. Fourteen interviews a day is not what it's about. I want to be on stage all the time, on telly all the time. It's insane: I sleep, eat, do my school work and dress in the same room!'

Melody Maker warned: 'It's not difficult to see the girl cracking up. She's not as steely as Kylie, not as streetwise as All Saints. And being solo, it's not like she has any bandmates to complain to.'

Her need for friendship, guidance and support was becoming critical. One journalist recalls: 'I remember going to a shoot and she'd been out the night before. No one said, "Billie's hung-over," but it was alluded to, and she was saying, "I'm so tired, I was out last night."

'It was like someone much older was talking, you almost forgot how young she was, and then all of a sudden she'd go back to being girly – she'd say to one of her aides, "Can we just stay in tonight and have some nice food, please? Would you just cook me something nice? Please?" It was really childish, the way she said it – I think she was exhausted, and she desperately wanted to be mothered and looked after, and it hit me, "You're a really young girl in a really scary industry."'

Scary was about to become terrifying.

4 WORLDWIDE WONDER

Innocent Records were not the only pop outfit to look at the success of the Spice Girls in 1997 and ask how that formula could be reapplied to the Top Ten. Bob and Chris Herbert were a father-and-son team who had brought the Spice Girls together three years earlier with an ad placed in *The Stage*.

Victoria, Geri and the other girls quickly realized they didn't need the Herberts to run their careers, and dumped the pair long before recording 'Wannabe'. Bob and Chris were determined to try again – and so another ad was placed. This one appealed for young male singers and dancers with 'edge and attitude' to audition for a boy band.

One of the 3,000 hopefuls who turned up was Scott Robinson, a friend of Billie's from drama school. Another was Richard Neville Dobson, who called himself Ritchie Neville and came from Solihull, near Birmingham. A former choirboy who was into grunge rock, Ritchie's appearance was striking: with wide-open eyes and a grin as broad as a ventriloquist's dummy's, he looked like he'd wandered off the set of a silent movie.

With three other boys, Scott and Ritchie became Five – or, as they sometimes spelled it, 5ive. Though the band didn't have a number-one hit until their eighth single – 'Keep On Movin'' in 1999 – they immediately won a hysterically loyal following among girls as young as seven, and when Billie first shared a bill with the boys, as an unknown at the Hammersmith Odeon for MTV in March 1998, she knew the audience were not remotely interested in her. They wanted Scott, Abs, J and Sean … and most of all they wanted Ritchie.

It was inevitable that Billie would keep bumping into the boys as their frenetic gigging schedules criss-crossed. It was just as inevitable that one of them would make a pass. When Ritchie started chatting to her back-stage at a gig in Germany, her first thought was that the other boys had urged him to do it for a bet.

She was flattered by his interest, though. He was good-looking and he talked to her as an equal, instead of the way most men treated her – she was thoroughly fed up with the star-struck celeb-spotters, the predators with false, fixed grins and the leery, condescending uncle types.

And Ritchie knew how it felt to be the act, the turn, the one on stage. To everybody else, Billie sometimes felt, she was a commodity. Everyone knew how to sell her, but no one understood what it was to be her. But Ritchie did. As they chatted at the bar, at first warily

'Because We Want To': fifteen-year-old Billie explodes on to the pop scene with her debut single, shooting straight to number one.

The campaign trail: 1998 is jam-packed with promotional work, including the Radio One Roadshow (*above right*, with DJ Chris Moyles).

Below: The strain begins to show.

Billie performing at the *Smash Hits* Poll Winners' Party. She was crowned Best Female Solo Star, but also voted overall Sad Loser Of '98.

Billie at the BRIT Awards, February 1999. She hated the outfit.

'I'm so in love I don't know what to do with myself,' Billie said of her relationship with Five singer Ritchie Neville. Here they attend the premiere of *Star Wars: Episode I – The Phantom Menace*.

All grown up: the year 2000, and Billie is back with a new single and a hot new look.

Opposite page: Billie, aged seventeen, at an after-show party at London club Sugar Reef. There was growing concern about the young star's party-loving lifestyle.

'Don't put your daughter on the stage': an ironic slogan, or a cry for help?

and then increasingly absorbed in each other's conversation, Billie realized she was meeting someone who saw the world from her own unreal perspective – a teenager packaged for ten-year-olds.

He knew how exhausting it was, how dangerous it sometimes felt. All his privacy, like hers, had been stripped away. He didn't have a personal life, he scarcely existed beyond the rehearsals and the signings and the travelling and the concerts. He knew there were days when he loved it and days when he didn't have time to feel any emotion at all.

With a lurch of surprise, Billie realized she had made a friend. A year ago, it would have been the most natural thing in the world to do. Now it was exceptional. None of her friends in Swindon could relate to what was happening in her life and most of her friends from stage school were simply envious. The worst of them were selling stories to the tabloids and the rest weren't speaking to her.

Worse still, she couldn't talk to her parents, who ran her fan club and managed her finances. They were remote and awkward, like peasants in a fairy tale who discover, to their bafflement, that the little girl they raised as a baby was really an enchanted princess.

Her only confidantes were the paid PAs and press officers, and the record company hangers-on who picked the clubs and restaurants every night and pressed glasses of wine into her hands. None of them cared much what she said: they listened to her, they said 'Yes' and 'No' when they should, but they didn't remember conversations the next day. Mostly, they didn't remember them the next minute.

Ritchie was different. He was listening. He was sharing her emotions. He could see the real person inside the package. And he was good-looking.

He was also a boy-band star, in a foreign country, with a drink in his hand. Billie liked him, but she didn't let her guard down too low. 'I did fancy him straight off, but I had it in my mind that he was in a boy band and you know what they're like. They have as many girls as they can,' she later said to reporter John Dingwall.

Billie and Ritchie didn't see each other again for eight weeks. The non-stop success story of Billie's pop career took precedence. Her remarkable achievements were underlined by her appearance at the BRITs that spring, the award ceremony that is the music industry's equivalent of the BAFTAs. As well as performing, she was nominated in two categories – Best British Female and Best British Newcomer. Though she didn't win, the fact that she was being recognized spoke volumes for her critical success as well as her commercial appeal.

'I was absolutely terrified performing at the BRIT Awards,' she told Christine Davies of the *Sunday People*. 'It was such a huge event and I knew there were going to be loads of people there watching me and also at home on TV. I was shaking like a leaf beforehand – but once I was up on stage I was fine.'

Her schedule had become dizzying. At first it had been hard to keep track of the days. Now it was a challenge to keep track of the continents. In February she flew to Japan for two days of non-stop promotional work, after a lightning visit to Taiwan. Just reading her schedule is tiring; living it was draining.

Arriving at her Tokyo hotel in the small hours on a Wednesday morning, she slept through breakfast and struggled through the jet lag while her make-up aide did her hair, her wardrobe assistant dressed her and her public relations adviser talked her through the protocols of dealing with Japanese interviewers.

Her father was in the next room, but there was no time to see him before the bus came to take her to EMI Japan's headquarters in Tokyo. This was the first time Paul Piper had joined his daughter on a trip abroad, mostly out of a growing unease at the pressures surrounding her. When they touched down at Narita international airport outside Tokyo, he had looked as bewildered as she felt.

EMI's executives had put on a welcome, with everyone leaving their office cubicles to bow to her. Billie struggled not to laugh, scared of doing or saying something inappropriate in the face of this excessive politeness. After a string of introductions to people whose names she couldn't understand, Billie was led back to the bus – so many people travelled with her that a limo wouldn't have been large enough. More often than not, Billie would sit with her PA, Deborah, who seemed like a pop version of the Victorian governess. Ten years older than Billie, she told people that the pair of them got on well because she could 'remember what it's like to be sixteen'.

What Deborah Lynam couldn't remember, of course, was how it felt to be a sixteen-year-old sales machine whose travelling companion was an employee appointed as Official Best Friend. In a movie, the two of them might have struck up an unlikely but heart-warming friendship. In reality, they were aliens, reduced to killing time with pastiches of teenage games, like thumbing through magazines to point at ugly men and ask, 'Would you snog him?'

At 2 p.m. Billie was recording a TV show called *Daibetteki*, starring Sonic the Hedgehog. It was a manic Japanese version of Saturday morning kids' TV. Her dressing room was hidden down hundreds of metres of corridors, and it was already occupied – by a stuffed toy, the Hello Kitty character Billie had seen every-where since arriving in Japan. This one was almost as big as she was.

Daibetteki's host, who the PR people had described as 'the Chris Evans of Tokyo', put his head round the door to introduce himself by pointing to his foot and saying, 'Hello, my name's Shoe. I am so famous you wouldn't believe it.' Billie greeted him with her best stage-school grin. Inside she was fighting hysterical laughter.

The show was frantic and incomprehensible. It featured a pair of comedians, billed as 'the funniest people in Japan'. Their only joke was to hit each other around the head with everything that came to hand as they tried to swat an invisible mosquito. Twenty girls from the audience were picked for a competition where they had to describe to Billie, through a translator, a traditional Japanese object or ritual. 'There was loads of screaming, giggling and jumping up and down,' commented a baffled Billie, who played along gamely.

The competition winner's prize was a trip to London to meet Billie's choreographer and learn her dance routines. No one in the entourage knew anything about this, least of all the choreographer.

Four hours of radio interviews followed the show, the same litany of questions she had to answer every time she arrived in a new country – which was currently happening twice a week. All her answers had to be filtered through a translator, and the process seemed endless. The promotion was working, though: at lunchtime she'd been an unknown in Japan, but by 9 p.m., when her aides took her shopping in the late-night, neon-powered Shibuya centre, people were approaching her for autographs. The Japanese way of demanding an autograph is the opposite of the Western method: in Tokyo, fans are hesitant and polite as they approach, and then scream and swoon when they get what they want. In Britain and America, they scream or yell first, and might say thank you afterwards.

Billie was hungry, but she didn't want to risk traditional Japanese food and the plastic imitations of food that represent menus in Tokyo were turning her stomach. Shortly before midnight they stumbled into a Burger King, after two hours of window-shopping for clothes – Billie liked the duffel coats that everyone was wearing in Tokyo that season and fancied getting one for her visit to Canada the following week.

There was no lie-in till lunchtime the next day: she had to be with her private tutor, Liz, at 9 a.m. for school studies. Her parents were still determined that she would sit at least three GCSEs that summer, in maths, art and English. That never happened: she ended up sitting lesser exams in the autumn, and barely scraping passes. Part of the problem was motivation: no one was going to buy her records on the basis of her exam results. But mostly it was exhaustion. Billie was living her career more intensely than even she, in her most ambitious daydreams, had believed possible. She simply didn't have any energy to spare for Liz, algebra and spelling tests.

After a scrambled meal, the bus whisked Billie and her aides – many of them looking jaded, jet-lagged or hung-over – back to EMI Japan's offices. There were no genuflections from the cubicles this time, just a string of interviewers from magazines to meet and the same questions over and over.

By 3 p.m. she was being shown around Tokyo by three presenters posing as fans for a TV show called *CD Groove XXX*. Her father was with her for part of the shoot, until they arrived at Kiddyland, an eight-storey toy shop, where Paul decided to go shopping for presents for Charlie, Harley and Ellie.

Outside HMV Billie stopped and gaped. Her album cover was on display … forty feet high. It was twice the size of a house.

She finally found a duffel coat she liked in Takeshita Street, and ate a meal for the cameras. It was easy to find energy to perform, to be bouncy and smiley and happy – pointing a camera at her was like plugging her into the mains. It wasn't so easy to swallow the octopus on her chopsticks.

The presenters took her to a karaoke bar with fifty private booths with microphones, where customers could rehearse. Then they set up the cameras in a park where it was five degrees below freezing and local youngsters were practising dance routines. They shot an impromptu version of 'Because We Want To' and wound up at 8 p.m., but the day wasn't over for Billie: she had a meal to attend with EMI executives. 'I get a bit homesick when I'm away,' she once admitted to a *Top of the Pops* magazine writer. There was never any time to address that, though.

The next day she was in Miami, Florida, to start shooting the video for 'Honey To The B', her next single, which would be released in April. Like her third hit, 'She Wants You', it was a track from her album and would not reach number one: both songs charted at number three in the UK.

Hello! magazine joined her at Key West, where she was enjoying the sunshine and glad to be away from bizarre game shows and manic presenters. 'It's like paradise. Everyone is so chilled and laid-back. But I think if you lived here for a long time you'd lose sense of normality,' she said.

Before her career, she had been on family trips to France and Spain: 'Now I seem to be away most of the time. I'm seeing a great deal of the world.'

But living out of a suitcase had stopped being fun. 'I find that really hard. I hate always seeing my clothes folded up in a case. It's difficult to keep sane when you're just travelling around all the time. If I know I'm going to be in a hotel room for a while, I try to put things around the room to make it more homely. I always put out photos of my family. A year ago, to stay in the luxury hotels I do now would have been amazing – I'd never have left the room, I'd have just sat there the whole time and looked around. Now, though, I can be staying in a hotel but I'm hardly ever there. It's just a room to sleep in.' And then, remembering to sound upbeat, she added, 'But it's lovely too.'

5 THE TIDE TURNS

After Florida, it was Los Angeles, Canada and then New York. She came home to Britain in March, where Ritchie was waiting to see her again. Uncertain of her feelings, she refused to go out with him at first, but he was persistent and he seemed genuine.

'I thought he'd just see me once, so I took a lot of convincing,' she admitted a year later to John Dingwall. 'He kept phoning me and telling me, "It's all sincere. I want to go out with you."'

The pair met up again back on British soil. Billie was hesitant to trust him: Ritchie's job meant girls were throwing themselves at him day in and day out, and Billie was reluctant to date someone who could have any girl he wanted with just a casual click of his fingers. But as she and Ritchie grew closer, her doubts began to fade.

'It was more the friendship at first. I had a chaperone at the beginning, but after a while everybody realized that I was old enough to take care of myself. People realized that I was able to deal with a pop lifestyle, which meant I could easily deal with a boyfriend. The first date we had was when I had just finished doing a *Live & Kicking* appearance [on children's TV] and I had arranged to meet him and his mum. We went shopping in Knightsbridge. Then I went back to my parents' in Swindon and we called each other from then on.'

The Sun broke the news of their relationship in March, and the backlash shocked them both. What seemed natural to their families – two lonely teenagers in the same careers becoming friends – was an outrage to their fans. And millions of tabloid readers who couldn't have cared less about their music saw a pair of spoiled brats, cynically manoeuvring into a brighter patch of limelight.

The agony columns of pop magazines were bristling with enraged adolescents. 'My friend and I heard that Billie and Ritchie are dating, and we think it's absolutely disgusting,' complained one fan in the April edition of *Big!* magazine. 'She's far too young for him and we think Ritchie can do better.'

Lisa, who signed herself an 'ex-Ritchie fan', warned: 'More people hate Billie and less people like Ritchie because of this.'

'It started to affect her health massively,' said a journalist who knew her well. 'She was so stressed. The people who should have stepped in to help were just having too much fun, hanging out at parties. At that age, most girls just want to be the popular girl at school – she was the popular girl in the whole country, which must have been an amazing feeling. And then for the backlash to start – and it was really extreme when it came – she went from being the nation's golden girl to public enemy number one. It wasn't just Five fans who hated her – a lot of people turned, because it was no longer cool to like her.

'To an adult that's really hard – to pick up a paper and see yourself being slated. To do a show and have everyone booing you. For a young girl, who has had nothing but praise, to suddenly be faced with this vitriol … And teenage girls can be some of the scariest people. Forget the adults, it's the teenage girls. They used to terrify me so I can imagine she must have been petrified to go anywhere – but she still had all these commitments in her diary which were probably booked the year before which she had to do, concerts and road-shows. To face these girls day after day, it must have been terrifying for her.'

To call it 'hatred' was no exaggeration. Poisonous letters, including death threats, started to arrive at the record company and the fan club, which was run by Paul and Mandy Piper from the family home. One girl threatened to throw an axe at Billie's head if she saw her in the street. After that, the Pipers handed over the running of the club to Innocent Records.

One teen magazine writer explained: 'She was origi-nally one of them, the girl-next-door who came from nothing and did well. Then it seemed like she turned her back on the fans, that she was only out for herself. The fans idolize those boys. They get very jealous. We had letters saying, "We hate Billie, she's a bitch." We had so many that we ended up not opening them.'

Billie called it, 'Absolutely unbelievable. Anyone would find that hard to deal with. It was rough for a few weeks, really scary. Ritchie's fans saw me as some kind of threat. They were just mixed up.'

Years later, she admitted the pressure had driven her to suicidal thoughts. Describing her mood at sixteen as 'mad, neurotic and self-destructive', she told the *Radio Times* in June 2006 that 'I had a very dark moment when I didn't want to be here any more, but I did nothing about it, thank God.' The support of Ritchie and her parents saved her – 'but it could have gone either way'.

It wasn't only Billie who suffered. Her mother, shaken by the hate mail and frustrated at the hold other people exercised over her sixteen-year-old daughter, voiced her worries to a reporter from the *Sunday People*. She was shocked to see her comments sensationalized under lurid headlines: 'Billie: She's worrying her mother silly … I fear my pop girl, sixteen, will lose her virginity, be tempted by drugs [and] become an anorexic.'

Mandy, who was just twenty-three when Billie was born, was quoted as fretting: 'I don't get to see my daughter a great deal any more. I am proud of her, but I can't help worrying about her. She is so young.'

The words were innocently meant. Billie still visited her mum and dad, though not as often as any of them would have liked. They talked on the phone, and Billie had given Mandy repeated promises that she was not taking drugs or partying too hard. Her mum was worried and that was normal: it's what mums do.

But most mums share their worries over the garden fence or with colleagues, not with tabloid reporters. With emotive words picked out in bold capitals or italics and the interview sandwiched between two pictures of Billie (one a school photo, the other posed in full make-up at the BRIT Awards, and the pair of them captioned, 'From this … To this'), the tone of Mandy's words became hysterical.

The whole piece read like a desperate last plea from an estranged parent who was waging an argument through the last resort, the pages of the press.

Though Mandy said that she was pleased for Billie that she'd achieved the success she'd always dreamed of, she also confessed, 'Sometimes I wish it had never happened.' At the end of the day, Billie was still Mandy's little girl. And Mandy was agonizing over the drugs that might be offered to Billie now that she was in the grown-up world of the music industry – not only recreational drugs, but also pick-me-ups to boost her energy for her stage performances. As a concerned mother, Mandy had obviously spoken to Billie at length about the dangers of drugs. But the young girl was on her own in London – and anything could happen.

'It's very difficult for her, coping with all this stardom. But we are all here for her if it ever gets too much. I won't let her lose track of reality. When she comes home, I'll say, "Billie, fill the dishwasher up," and she'll say, "What?" As soon as I see her getting like that, I say, "Oh, sorry, you're a star, aren't you?"'

Billie's fondness for burgers and fries was well known, so the paper's claim that she had an 'obsession with her weight' seemed contrived. She was on record as hating the red spandex one-piece which she wore to the BRITs, because she thought it made her look huge next to the elfin girls from B★Witched. She'd even called her mum to moan about it. But she can't have been too concerned, because after the show she walked into a late-night corner shop to buy a few essentials. 'I was in this big dress with all this hair,' she laughed, 'and people were obviously thinking, "What is she doing?"'

Mandy, however, appeared to deliver obliging quotes about looming anorexia: 'She thinks she looks massive. Every time I see her she asks me, "Do I look fat?"' Though Mandy always set her daughter's mind at rest, with Billie being far away from home, it was difficult to know if Mandy's reassurances actually sank in. The worried mum had noticed that her daughter had slimmed down recently, but was quick to say that she'd take action if Billie ever took her dieting to extremes.

On the relationship with Ritchie, she sounded more relaxed. He clearly got the thumbs-up from Billie's mum and Mandy was also confident that the young lovers were well suited, partly because they were both experiencing the heady – and sometimes hostile – world of pop stardom.

What Billie thought about this in-depth interview is unknown: she kept silent in the wake of the *Sunday People* splash. At any rate, she was too busy to react publicly, being whisked away to America again for more promotional engagements. Her first US single, 'She Wants You', went on sale across the States in April, peaking at number nine in the Hot Dance chart; the album was released in mid-May and eventually placed on the Heatseekers album chart at number seventeen. In June, she performed 'Because We Want To' at the New York Giants football stadium at the start of a football tournament – the Women's World Cup.

The concert was the biggest of her life, in front of an audience of 100,000 that included President Bill Clinton. Billie was more impressed by actress Jennifer Lopez, heading the bill in her pop star persona, J-Lo. The organizers had picked 'Because We Want To' as the tournament's theme tune to underline the idea that women could enjoy playing soccer as much as men. 'It doesn't really represent football specifically,' Billie admitted, 'but it's about being young and enjoying yourself and I think it ties in with women's football. Females can play what is typically seen as a male sport. There's such a passion about the game.'

She told *Shoot* magazine that she didn't follow the sport – 'but whenever there's a big England game on, I'll always try to watch it.' Ritchie, on the other hand, was a fan of Aston Villa, his home-town club, and he was threatening to make her join him on the terraces at Villa Park. 'Ritchie really wants me to go watch a game, and I'm totally up for it.'

She was being brave even to contemplate going out in public with Ritchie. At the *Smash Hits* awards, she had been subjected to catcalls and jeers from the moment she stepped on to the stage. The Five fans were unforgiving, not to say downright cruel, and they treated Billie like a pantomime villain. It would have been funny if it hadn't been so frightening.

'It was the Poll Winners' Party, and she was so dev-astated about that,' recalled a journalist who was there. 'She was crying backstage afterwards.'

If there was any single moment when Billie Piper decided that being a pop star was no fun any more, that was it. 'It's an emotional thing – any girl would get upset about that. And all I want to know is, why? I've never had a chance to ask, but if I did meet the girls that did that, I'd ask, "What have I done to upset you?"'

Billie honoured her schedule for a few more weeks, with the US trip, but she made it plain to her record company that she needed a break. She was exhausted, her sales were drooping and she was turning into a national hate figure. 'The people at [Innocent] were fantastic. They just said, "She needs time off," and gave me as much time as I wanted,' she said to the *Express*.

To emphasize how set she was on regaining control of her life, she sacked her manager, Steve Blackwell, later in the year and hired Nick Godwin and Nicki Chapman, the team behind S Club 7. 'People do take liberties,' she told reporters in Scotland, 'but that's when you have to call the shots and I've learned how to do that. It's hard for a woman to be ruthless without being called a bitch. Men can be ruthless and they're just called productive.'

Looking back in 2006, Billie felt her work schedule had been a 'work-you-to-death' regime which had made her 'exhausted and bitter'. And without pointing the finger at anyone, she complained that she'd been 'young, green and taken advantage of ... although I was working twice as hard as I am now, I was left with hardly any money.'

The US tour had strengthened her determination to take a career break. For twelve months she had barely had a day to herself and the cost had been high: illness, shattered friendships and ugly rumours. Now she had found a friend who could share her stresses and understand them – but their jobs were keeping them continents apart. It was unbearable.

'At the beginning it was terrible being apart so much – it was like forever pining and just feeling sick all the time,' she told the *Express*. 'You can't get enough, moderation goes out the window, you're just being so greedy, you want more and more. I went away to America for a couple of months and that was just hell – but, actually, that helped us to deal with how the relationship is now. In the end, we just have to handle it because that's our jobs.'

That last comment sounds like the weary resignation of a thirty-five-year-old who knows her husband must work evenings and weekends if they're going to keep paying the mortgage. She was only sixteen, but nothing about her lifestyle betrayed it.

'The whole thing that surrounded Billie was grown-up,' one pop journalist commented. 'She probably felt a lot older than her years. She didn't think about the fact the thing with Ritchie might not last – she was just completely swept away with it. They were like a couple ten years older, in the way they acted around each other. For most people, if you're fifteen or sixteen and you're going out with someone, you'll see them once or twice a week – bump into them at school and look really embarrassed, or see them at the park. But they were going to premieres and fancy restaurants: it was like they had fast-forwarded to doing the proper grown-up thing. They didn't have a chance to go on normal dates to the cinema, because it was all showbizzy stuff. They seemed really serious – they had kept it quiet for quite a long time, but once it came out it did cause her a lot of problems.

'She was completely full-on with Ritchie. I remember they went to the premiere of the Star Wars movie, *The Phantom Menace*. They looked like a proper couple. Then they went to a musical in the West End, *Boyband*. It wasn't like they were just starting to go out with one another and they had time to get to know one another. Because everyone wanted to know what was going on. Ritchie had so many fans, so it was such a big thing for them to go to this premiere and be seen. She was putting herself at real risk. People in the industry knew they were seeing each other, but at first they were denying it. They seemed so grown up, but I remember thinking, "She's so young – it probably won't last five minutes, and she's putting herself through this."'

The tabloids reacted by demanding to know when she and Ritchie would start a family. They sniffed a celebrity wedding, a teenage edition of Posh 'n' Becks: David Beckham's girlfriend, Victoria, had given birth to their first child in March. 'I'm not going to have babies and get married,' Billie protested. 'That's a long way off.'

The emotional strain was also telling on her health. Ever since her stomach illness before Christmas, she had been prone to viruses and debilitating infections that preyed on her exhaustion. Three appearances had been cancelled, and once again Billie was forced to dispel rumours that something worse had happened than a mere tummy upset or sore throat.

'It was just flu and tonsillitis and it came at the wrong times,' she told *Mirror* reporter Jan Disley. 'I fly a lot and I'm always kissing fans and holding their hands. I'm not suggesting they're full of germs but you're bound to pick up everything going. There is also a lot to cope with. It's emotionally and physically draining. I spent the first year worrying about what people thought, and concentrating on How To Be A Pop Star. I forgot about my own needs. Now I'm just plodding along. I've decided to learn my craft and just enjoy my job.'

Wedding rumours intensified when Billie and Ritchie were spotted wearing matching rings. The story went round that engraved on the inside of each ring were the words '*ad aeternitatem*' – 'to eternity'. It wasn't as emphatic as David Beckham's gesture of having his family's names tattooed on to his torso, but it added another layer of credibility to the notion that Billie would soon be a bride.

She didn't do much to dispel the rumours. 'I'm so in love I don't know what to do with myself,' she told Ian Hyland of the *Sunday Mirror*. 'I'm all keyed up. I can't explain it. It's so cool being with Ritch, even though I hardly ever see him. It's difficult fitting time in between his schedule and my own diary, but we talk all the time and when we do [see each other] we make the most of it.'

The couple had established a bedtime routine, where they would phone from wherever they were in the world, in whatever time zone, to wish each other good-night before falling into bed. Increasingly, that meant Ritchie would be calling from Europe, Japan or America to chat with Billie as she sat up in bed at the London apartment where she was now living on her own. She'd bought it from her earnings, with her parents' sanction, for £200,000, and after initial discussions about sharing it with an aide or even a parent, she had opted to live there alone. As she pointed out, she had been largely on her own and coping in London since she was twelve.

When Five weren't on tour, Billie and Ritchie would see family in Solihull or Swindon. 'He comes to my mum's house in Swindon,' she said, 'and takes my ten-year-old brother Charlie out for a spin in his car, which makes Charlie love me even more. Then we'll go to the pictures or out to dinner. Just normal stuff, really.'

Her life was so far from normal, though, that she couldn't even walk into McDonald's with her boyfriend without being simultaneously jostled for autographs and jeered at. Walking down the street amid a sea of photographers always made her blush, she told the *Radio Times*, while the movie-premiere experience was horrible: 'I hate walking up those bloody red carpets. It stresses me out massively. My hands get really clammy.' Luckily, her seventeenth birthday party wasn't the huge showbiz affair that had knocked her backwards at sixteen. Like many girls her age the major present that day was a car, but hers was not a banger renovated by her dad, but a new Ford Ka from her record company. She wasn't even planning to take driving lessons.

Other seventeen-year-olds weren't expected to be role models to millions of youngsters or to solve people's worries with a letter and a piece of personal advice. 'I get loads of letters from fans and they talk to me about their problems. I try to give them advice from my own experience. But I'm still growing up myself so I'm hardly qualified, am I?'

She was decisively rejecting the pressure to be a spokeswoman for her generation, saying to the *Sunday Mirror*, 'I don't want to get involved in that kind of thing, because things you say have a habit of catching up with you. Imagine if I say, "Don't smoke, kids," and someone takes a picture of me holding a cigarette.'

And if she wasn't going to be a spokeswoman, and her boyfriend's fans were booing her off the stage at awards ceremonies, and every Sunday supplement guide to 'What's Cool' placed her on the far side of 'What's Not', it was time to drop out of sight.

6 BACK IN BUSINESS

When she came back, in March 2000, she had a new look, a new single and her surname. Little pop wonder Billie was now tougher, chilled-out Billie Piper. The girl who'd shot to fame as an instant single-name icon, aping Madonna, had grown up enough to be herself: her full name, she said, was 'nothing to be ashamed of'.

Her hair was darker, her clothes were chic, her sound was funkier and she had even co-written some of the songs on her new album, penning lyrics. The break had been all about 'enjoying the taste of reality', she told interviewers, and 'experimenting with my look', watching TV and doing nothing. 'I became completely addicted to Richard and Judy [on daytime TV]. And then I watched anything else that happened to be on.'

That insouciance lasted until about halfway through the first interview. It was clear that the traumas of 1999 had left her scarred and she needed to talk about them. It was also clear she was terrified of blundering into the same minefield.

'It's hard when your job is to get up on a stage and perform, if you're too scared to do it,' she said frankly to the *Express*. The fear had been so bad, she revealed, that her dentist had prescribed gum shields to stop her from grinding her teeth as she slept. She chewed right through them. 'It's been a pretty stressful time,' she admitted to *Heat* magazine in another interview, 'but then I guess I'm a pretty stressful type of person. I am slowly getting more confident as I get older, but I still do suffer from a lot of inferiority complexes.'

That was a jarring statement from such a seasoned performer. The sustained hostility from the press and ex-fans had stripped away much of her self-belief. 'I've gone through so much,' she said. 'I've travelled the world and I've met a lot of incredible people. But it's also been really hard. I've come in for more abuse than you could imagine.

'I really love being in the public eye but it can be really difficult. All I ever wanted was for people to love me, but I've been on the receiving end of an awful lot of jealousy and spite. The papers have been really, really nasty. I spent so many hours crying on the phone to my mum, asking her what I'd done wrong.'

Billie could not see how newspapers that had been supportive and positive could have turned on her so abruptly; she didn't understand why journalists who had seemed friendly and full of praise could write up an interview with such malice. 'I'm trying to bring happiness to people, but the papers are just trying to bring me down ... Some of the stuff people say is so ridiculous, like that I'm sleeping with my manager and taking loads of drugs. I mean, I've been married about four times! To be honest, it really gets to me. These people have never met me, they don't know me and yet they seem determined to ruin my career and my life. Well, they can piss off, quite frankly.'

Billie was also still deeply hurt that so many people she'd known in Swindon were ready to betray her friendship for a few hundred pounds. As she told the *Express*: 'My friends were selling stories to the newspapers, and I realized that people I really loved could just shit on me. They did it for money. My friends were wise enough not to be tricked and they knew what tabloids were like. I knew they'd got money for it and I was gutted.'

It was hard for her to understand her own motives for a comeback. She had found the strength to get out of the spotlight, and she knew it would be dangerous to go back – dangerous for her health, her sanity and her personal safety. It wasn't even as if she liked the perks of celebritydom. She openly criticized the Met Bar, saying that despite the hype the paparazzi had built up about the trendy venue, the place was gloomy and quiet, with no one talking to each other because it wouldn't be funky to do so. 'It's so lame and crap and boring!' she exclaimed. 'It's so much better to go down your local pub and have a right good chuckle.'

Her attitude to eating out was the same. Forget The Ivy and The Fat Duck – Billie was a greasy-spoon kind of girl. She was also fond of takeaways, especially in front of a movie. 'Those are my favourite times. You're not trying to be anyone you're not, you're not out being a star.'

So why come back? Part of her missed the adrenaline surge. She had been performing ever since she was four, and when she turned on the TV to see America's teen stars, Britney Spears and Jessica Simpson, she was envious. But more than that, she didn't want to be scared away by people she didn't respect. 'I know how the media works now and I know how to look after myself.'

Most of all, she saw Ritchie's career growing stronger. He had survived newspaper viciousness with the support of his bandmates. Billie had been on her own – but this time, she would have Ritchie, a man she described as being 'so not starry'. With a down-to-earth boyfriend at her side, one who spurned showbiz parties and was 'straight down the line', as she put it, Billie would be fine.

With his help, she was learning to see the world in a harsher, more cynical light – the way she would have to approach it, if she was to cope this time round. 'I can see through people, or I like to think I can. It seems like a terrible loss of innocence, but then I've got so much love to give people that I really let people in, and Ritch has taught me not to do that so much, because it only ends in tears and gets me into trouble … I love holding people and hugging them, and I've probably confused a lot of boys in the past, but I never realized until Ritchie pointed it out.

'I'm definitely a one-man woman – I've never been one for that whole "different boy every week" thing. I like a real, solid relationship. I'm very much like my mother, who's only ever had two boyfriends in her life.'

She also credited her parents for their support and regretted that at stage school she'd grown apart from them. In her early teens, she had rarely told them anything about her life – who her friends were, what she enjoyed about London, the ways she planned to become famous. 'Now I tell them everything. I have to because I've no one else I can totally trust.'

There was one other love in her life – a chocolate Labrador puppy called Milo. He was her Christmas present from Ritchie and he shared her apartment in London. Five months old, he had captivated Billie's attention and she lavished affection on the young pup. She also enjoyed the responsibility of looking after him, saying it made her 'less selfish'.

Everyone wanted to know if she and Ritchie would marry, but Billie was being wary, citing their youth and expressing only a careful confidence in the relationship's future. But she was confident on one aspect of their partnership: 'The good thing is that, if we ever do split up, I'm sure we will always be good friends because we're neither of us the kind of people to hold a grudge.'

She didn't know it, but that split was only weeks away.

The Sun's headline broke the story: 'After eighteen months Ritchie ended it with a phone call … I'm empty inside.'

Billie told showbiz editor Dominic Mohan the call from Ritchie, who was on tour, came out of the blue; that he'd announced their relationship was no longer working and he wanted to end it. Shocked, Billie had agreed. She was clinging to the hope that, when career pressures subsided, they might get back together. 'I feel numb and heartbroken, but luckily haven't got time to sit down and dwell on it. I am gutted though.'

Neither of them had anyone else in their lives, she said, and she was determined not to rush into another romance. The hardest parts were going to bed without that nightly chat on the phone and knowing that the joint birthday party they had planned for September – his twenty-first, her eighteenth – was cancelled.

The story fitted with everything she'd been telling the press for weeks, that the lack of privacy in their goldfish-bowl affair was hard to bear. 'We're so accessible to people's lives, it's almost as if we're not real people – we're not allowed to have real lives or real emotions.'

At first, Ritchie said nothing. Then, as the stories spread of how callously he'd dumped her, he hit back: Billie was the one who ended the relationship, he claimed, and she'd done it with a text message. His friends put the word about that her record company had told her to use the break-up for publicity and sympathy sales: 'Day And Night', the comeback single, went straight to number one at the beginning of May.

Gossips linked Billie's name to actor Danny Dyer, star of the clubbing movie *Human Traffic*, and, days later, to Ralf Little, who played Antony in the BBC sitcom *The Royle Family*. *The Sun* claimed they had laughed and kissed all evening at a fashionable London bar, Abigail's Party, before leaving in the same taxi. By the middle of June, Ritchie was angry enough to start a public slanging match. Talking to Eva Simpson at the *Daily Star*, he called Billie a nag, announced he intended to 'have fun being a bachelor boy again' and added that the one he really missed was Milo the Labrador.

'She's been linked with a few people,' he said, 'and I wish her well. It won't be long for me, either. I'm looking forward to doing what bachelors do – going out with the lads and getting blotto.

'It's great not to worry about getting home before midnight and not having anyone to answer to. I've got my new flat now and there are no disputes about tidiness. I wasn't particularly messy, but she was a fanatic about tidiness – even though I did all the cooking. Now I can do what I want and not have to put up with all the nagging.'

Billie was horrified. 'The fact that we've split up is hard enough without it being splashed across the press,' she said to *The Daily Telegraph*. She tried to retreat to the inoffensive defence that work had driven them apart, that no one was to blame, but at the same time she was furious that people thought she'd engineered the split to sell her record.

'That's a horrible thing to suggest. I'd rather people didn't buy my record if they were just buying it because they felt sorry for me. When you break up with someone it's so sickening anyway, there's so much pain involved – why would I want the whole nation to know about it?'

She didn't speak to Ritchie for weeks after the break-up, and told friends she was shocked at how bitter it had become. The one person she had relied on to make the media pressure bearable had become her enemy. What happened next was as inevitable as the crash when a car suddenly loses its steering and its brakes.

Billie was 'drinking too much', as she admitted to the *Radio Times* in 2006: 'I never thought it was a problem – it's only with hindsight you realize you were a bit out of control. I still turned up for work, even though I had a face like a slapped arse.' She added that her eyes had felt lifeless and her smile false.

Three days after the *Star* ran Ritchie's interview, Billie went to Bar 38 in Covent Garden, a club for over-eighteens. She didn't buy drinks herself, but her older companions made repeated trips to the bar.

At about 11 p.m., after a visit to the toilets, she began shaking. Some onlookers claimed she was foaming at the mouth. Then she collapsed.

Her friends tried to revive her, but Billie was unconscious. Struggling to pick her up, they called out for help and one of the club-goers stepped in to lift her. He was later named as entertainments company director Adam Clarke, who was twenty-seven. He took quick action when Billie suddenly blacked out, scooping her up and rushing her out to her vehicle. Her companions then took over, assuring him that they would get her to hospital themselves. Adam gave his view on the fainting fit: 'I know she hadn't been drinking and I'm pretty sure it wasn't drugs.'

Few others were so kind with their comments. One witness claimed: 'One minute Billie was laughing and joking, the next she was on the floor struggling to breathe. Her friends were all panicking.'

'We saw her go off to the Ladies,' said a woman, 'and come back a few minutes later. Then all hell broke loose. She fell to the floor and lots of people went to help her. They were really panicking. I thought she was going to be sick. The poor girl didn't seem to know where she was or what was going on. It was very scary – I thought she was having a fit.'

Another said: 'She looked a complete mess. She was foaming at the mouth.' A fourth added, 'Her eyes were rolling around. She looked in a really bad way.'

Bar manager James Dunne told reporters: 'We can confirm that Billie fainted. It was all over very quickly and her friends didn't want to call an ambulance. She was drinking with friends. We can't say whether she drank too much.'

Her publicist, Dave Pitman, began an immediate effort to limit the damage, but almost every national newspaper in Britain, both the Sundays and the dailies, ran shock-horror stories which made much of Billie's frequent toilet visits.

'It's not drugs. That's definitely not the case,' said Pitman. 'She has got a mild kidney infection that is causing some discomfort, and she has been put on antibiotics. Because she fainted [the hospital is] keeping her in tonight, but they are hoping she will be out tomorrow. She is going to be fine.'

Billie added a statement of her own: 'It's been a bit of a shock, but I'm going to be OK. One minute I'm having fun with my mates, the next someone's carrying me out to my car. I'd like to thank the guy for acting so quickly and getting me out so I could get to hospital as soon as I did.'

Mandy Piper made the same calming noises. 'Billie's fine. She collapsed because she had a stomach complaint. If there was anything more serious, I'd be with her now and not at home. We're not worried.'

'She's fine, there's nothing to worry about,' her father echoed.

But clearly she wasn't fine, and a lot of people were rightly worried. A girl who is too young to buy alcohol should not be collapsing in a bar, even if a stomach bug was the cause.

Years later, in a *Radio Times* interview, Billie seemed to hint heavily that she *had* dabbled with drugs: 'I tried all those things, but it never became a problem. I was so green and that's what saved me – otherwise I may have got into it more because everyone else was and it seemed like fun.'

At the time, the repeated claims that she'd been back and forth to the loos all evening read like a coded accusation of drug-taking; a bar spokesman joined the chorus of voices insisting that was nonsense. Billie herself blamed her toilet trips on cystitis, a painful infection of the urinary tubes.

As the Sunday papers splashed the story across their front pages, Billie tried to deflect the rumours.

'Speaking faintly from her hospital bed,' as *The Sun* put it, Billie said: 'It has nothing to do with drugs – I don't do drugs. I've had this infection before and it may be a recurring thing when I'm run-down and tired.'

She named her heartache over the split with Ritchie as a contributing factor in her dramatic collapse. Under pressure from all angles, the painful break-up was the last straw for a vulnerable Billie. It had all been too much and everything came to a head that night in the bar.

She blamed her fame for the recurrent whispers about drug-taking. In the public eye from such a young age, she felt people were biding their time until she made an error, ready to pounce at the slightest hint of any impropriety. But she defended her right to go out and have a good time. She was, after all, a seventeen-year-old girl – and all seventeen-year-olds go out partying. Billie wanted to pursue these normal activities, but was well aware of the media's take on things and their interpretation that her socializing meant she was going off the rails.

She acknowledged that drugs were in evidence in the music industry, but stressed at the time that she was not caught up in that scene whatsoever: her illness and subsequent frailty caused the collapse. She described how the pain had initially hit her during the afternoon: the incident in the bar was the climax to an ongoing problem and not connected with anything she did on the night itself. She had even told her mates that she needed some medical attention – the pain, far from subsiding, had been getting worse. But her body cried out for help before she could reach a doctor: 'One minute I was talking to my friends, then I had the biggest head rush ever and I collapsed.'

The next day, *The Sun*'s showbiz editor, Dominic Mohan, ran an open letter to Billie, full of snide concern and double entrendres: 'The small matter of a hat-trick of number-one hits – that is nothing to be sniffed at.'

Mohan reminded her that he'd given her a cake and balloons at her sixteenth birthday party and told her piously to stop socializing in London; instead, she should be spending time with 'your young friends in Swindon'. If she didn't, she could end up as a 'showbiz casualty'.

The concern voiced by Julia Dickinson, Billie's former drama teacher from Bradon Forest Secondary School, was more real. 'She obviously needs time to relax and calm down, but I am sure there will be pressure on her to get back as soon as possible. If someone is not in the limelight for a while, they are soon forgotten about. I am very worried about her – there is a great burden on her to succeed. She clearly knows she has to appeal to a wider age group, and has to appear grown-up on and off stage. Maybe she should be allowed to be a normal girl for a while. I think people forget how young she is.'

Nine days later, Billie was back on stage, performing 'Day And Night' in front of an audience of 50,000 at Southern FM's Party In The Park in Brighton. And she was still on speaking terms with Mohan. 'I feel like I've been to hell and back,' she told him. 'But I feel great now. It's nice to perform again.'

Ritchie, meanwhile, had discovered he liked talking about life after Billie. At the beginning of July, he bragged (to Mohan, again): 'At first it was quite difficult to get back into the dating scene. It was weird to think about which clothes are best to go pulling in. I didn't need to do that when I was with Billie.'

Later in the month, he portrayed himself in the *Express* as lovesick. He'd adored Billie, he'd been head over heels about her and now they were just friends. 'It is really hard. It does my head in. We've both still got feelings and it's like it ended prematurely. I was away on a world tour ... We had a few little problems and it was like, "While I'm away, let's not call each other and when I get back we'll have a good old chat about everything." But when I got back it was over. I don't know what happened. I wish I did.'

That weekend, Five went to number one with 'We Will Rock You' and Ritchie and Billie met at ITV's studios to record *SM:TV*, Ant and Dec's Saturday morning show. They talked, and afterwards Ritchie announced, 'We had a great laugh. We're still very close and have a real chemistry between us. Everyone was looking at us to see how we reacted to each other – but we ignored that.'

Meanwhile, first boyfriend David Price discovered that his revelations were still in demand. He claimed Billie had been calling him, emotional and stressed, to pour out her heart. She would give up her career, her fame and her money, the video-shop assistant maintained, to turn back the clock and escape from the endless touring, interviews and promotional work. 'She knows she has sacrificed everything for her career,' he said to the *Sunday People*. 'She told me she'd ditch it all to get her old life back.'

He even claimed Billie wanted to revive their relationship and that when she was alone after shows in foreign hotels, she would call to ask if there was any chance they could get back together. Price was adamant that wouldn't happen, because 'she lives in a different world'. And he must have been telling the truth, because Billie and David Price never did get back together.

What did come back was her kidney infection. After shooting the BBC Saturday morning show *FBi* in Glasgow, Billie was doubled over with pain. Cancelling a concert with Ronan Keating and All Saints at Nottingham's City In The Park festival, she flew to London and saw a specialist in Harley Street. He advised her to get lots of rest and drink plenty of water, but within days she had flown to Canada on a promotional tour. 'She is right as rain again now – there is no big problem,' asserted a spokesman.

There was no let-up in the schedule. With another single, 'Something Deep Inside', out at the beginning of September and her second album, *Walk Of Life*, due later that month, Billie was booked to appear in Australia, New Zealand, Japan and across Europe before Christmas, with barely a day off. 'Half the time she doesn't even know what day it is, because she's so busy,' commented her voice coach, Izzy Cooper, a classical soprano.

On top of this, the hate mail and threatening phone calls continued. One woman's messages were so stomach-turning that the record company decided they had no choice but to contact the police. Five of the calls were traced to a flat in Canning Town, east London, and another to a public call box round the corner. A thirty-two-year-old woman was arrested and charged with three counts of threatening to kill Billie, one of harassment and one of sending malicious communications.

The magistrate at Horseferry Road seemed more concerned with playing the case for laughs. 'I don't know anything about Billie Piper,' commented Roger Davies, who was sixty. 'My knowledge of music stops at The Beatles.' But the woman, Juliet Peters, was remanded in custody, a move which meant the court thought she might be too dangerous to be released. Instead, she would remain under lock and key until her trial.

Even though 'Something Deep Inside' went to number four, Billie's eighteenth birthday celebrations that September felt hollow. Ritchie was on the guest list. 'We missed each other too much to be apart, but we're taking things real slow this time. I do still love him. We're lucky we remained so close after our split,' she told the *News of the World*. 'We couldn't just brush it under the carpet and hide our feelings. Now it's like seeing each other for the first time again.'

They teased each other for the press: Ritchie claimed he'd wanted to give Billie a car as a birthday present, but she couldn't drive. She retorted, 'He hasn't got me anything – typical guy!'

But the reunion was brittle, with Ritchie admitting, 'We're not back together. I love being with her, but we are trying to avoid the same mistakes we made the first time round.'

The celebration was held at Papa Gaio in Soho, with half the country's pop stars there: H from Steps, Kerry Katona and Natasha Hamilton from Atomic Kitten, TV presenter Dani Behr and a roomful of ex-house-mates from *Big Brother*, fresh from its inaugural season.

The Sun, which had provided a cake for her sixteenth, dumped an unwelcome layer of icing on it this time, by asking to turn up with a sniffer dog. His name was Charlie and he was trained to find cocaine. Like Billie's own pet, Milo, he was a Labrador, and he'd met Billie once before, at the BRITs. Then, she'd told reporters, 'He can sniff me all he wants.' This time he was unwelcome, but whether Charlie was turned away or given his own dog bowl of champagne, Billie couldn't win. 'Billie Bans *Sun* Sniff Dog,' screamed the front page.

'I heard all the rumours, they were always there, but she didn't seem at all like the kind of girl who would do loads of drugs,' one music journalist said. 'These stories followed her round, but I hope they're not true because I'd want nothing but good things for her – she was always just lovely.'

The non-stop demands on her brought her emotions to the surface. She was constantly criticizing herself, blaming her 'emotional, theatrical, dramatic' personality for her insecurities. 'I cry really easily,' she told reporter Desmond Sampson. 'Towards the end of my last tour I was crying nearly every day because I just wanted to go home. Only today, I thought, "I can't do this any more, because I don't feel well and I'm tired." I mean, when I go home I'm exhausted and I just spend a lot of my time recuperating. I enjoy having pressure on me, and I enjoy working hard, but it's late nights, end-on-end, and it's so tiring.'

The strain of being able to trust no one was also telling on her. 'I now realize I need to really grill everyone I meet before I make friends with them, to prevent any gossip. But in the long run I wonder if that's a bad thing, because maybe it'll make me a lonely person. I've become much more cynical too, which is probably my biggest fault. It's easy to have your head turned in this business and I admit that, at the start, I loved everyone and thought everyone loved me. But since I've been going out with Ritchie, I can see through people a lot easier now.'

The tone of that interview, early in November 2000, just after a video shoot in Scotland for what turned out to be her last single, made it clear she was barely coping. By 22 November, her health problems had returned and she pulled out of the BBC's *The John Daly Show* in Belfast, suffering from gastroenteritis.

At rehearsals for the *Smash Hits* Poll Winners' Party two weeks later, she broke down in the middle of a song. Eyewitnesses said she started shaking and slumped to the floor, sobbing, 'I just can't handle this any more.'

One onlooker said: 'Billie looked very pale and gaunt. She was shaking and looked like she was on the point of a breakdown. She kept saying she just couldn't carry on.'

Minutes later she left the studio with her mobile phone clamped to her ear.

However, she was well enough to appear on Chris Evans's breakfast show on Virgin Radio ten days later, on Wednesday 13 December. That was the day the rest of her life began.

⌐ HEAD OVER HEELS

When Billie walked into the studio for her interview with Chris Evans, she threw her arms around the host. 'When she arrived,' Chris said, a few days later, 'she gave me a hug which was a bit too tight and I thought, "Hang on, that wasn't the usual showbiz hug. What was all that about?" And that was the start of it, really.'

What it might have been about was Billie's self-confessed fondness for hugs, despite Ritchie's warnings that she had confused a lot of young men that way … but it's also likely she instinctively recognized someone who was as sick of showbiz as she was.

They had met once before, when she was a guest on his TV chat show. Their first encounter took place in the *TFI Friday* make-up room: Chris had stripped to the waist and his hairy chest had captivated Billie. She later told Piers Morgan, 'There was a definite mutual instant attraction.' The chemistry was plain to see on the show itself, too. Never one to be shy, during the interview Billie told Chris that she loved his shirt. He returned the compliment and the next thing viewers knew they were switching tops. Neither pursued the rapport at that time, however, as both were in relationships. But the initial spark didn't fade away.

Evans was a thirty-four-year-old media millionaire with a reputation for high-publicity romances with girl-friends including singer Kim Wilde, model Rachel Tatton-Brown, Spice Girl Geri Halliwell, actress Anna Friel, TV presenter Melanie Sykes and DJ Sara Cox. A successful TV producer and presenter, he was worth an estimated £70 million after selling his Ginger Media Group, which owned the Virgin station as well as pro-ducing his television vehicles, *Don't Forget Your Toothbrush* and *TFI Friday*, to Scottish Media Group in March 2000 for £285 million.

Chris had started out in London as a production assistant for Jonathan Ross, but the path which led him there was extraordinary. Born in Warrington, Cheshire, in 1966, his mother was a factory worker and his father a bookmaker. He was bullied at school for his gawky looks and ginger hair – in one mortifying attack, he was kicked to the ground by an older boy who urinated on his prostrate body. Chris was just thirteen when his father died; until then, he had been regarded as acade-mically promising. He was too traumatized even to attend the funeral and from then on his behaviour dete-riorated. School friends remember him exposing himself to the class during a geography lesson. That trait never left him: in later years he would sometimes enliven production meetings by pulling down his trousers, brandishing his genitals and exclaiming, 'What's that all about then?'

But even as a schoolboy he showed a flair for business. He would buy sweets wholesale and sell them to fellow pupils, undercutting tuck-shop prices. And his fondness for dropping his pants helped in one of his first jobs, as a strippergram, bursting into hen parties wearing nothing but a Tarzan loincloth.

In the mid-eighties, he had a daughter, Jade, with his then partner, Alison Ward. Around this time, he got his first job in radio, as a sidekick to an established DJ on Manchester's Piccadilly Radio. He was promoted, getting a show in his own right on the 'graveyard shift' between 2 a.m. and 6 a.m. But his taste for off-colour jokes upset listeners even at that time of the day and, after complaints about a feature on how to cook pets, he quit the station and moved to London. There, in 1991, he met and wed radio producer and presenter Carol McGiffin. The pair split acrimoniously after less than two years together.

Evans's talent for anarchic and unpredictable radio earned him notoriety at London's local BBC radio station, GLR, where he would appear at live gigs dressed only in a raincoat, with a banana sticking out of the front. Gags like that made him an outrageous success on Channel 4's *The Big Breakfast*, which he launched in 1992 with Gaby Roslin. The tabloids loved to hate him and the publicity for his next show was guaranteed. The first series to be made by his own company, Ginger Productions, it was a late-night game show on Channel 4 called *Don't Forget Your Toothbrush,* where contestants who humiliated themselves sufficiently could win a holiday overseas.

Radio 1 boss Matthew Bannister, who had employed Chris at GLR, hired him in 1995 to revive the breakfast slot, giving Ginger Productions unprecedented permission to run the show. Listening figures soared, and so did complaints: most of the banter on air, in a show traditionally popular with schoolchildren, was about drinking and casual sex. Another programme for Channel 4, the surreal chat show *TFI Friday*, made him the most famous man in the British media, even after he walked out of the BBC when his attempts to negotiate a four-day week failed.

In 1997 he made the leap from presenter to tycoon with the purchase of a controlling stake in Virgin Radio for £87.5 million, including £2 million of his own money and his 55 per cent of Ginger. He'd been presenting the morning show at Virgin for two months and on the morning the news broke he told listeners, 'It's great to be boss.'

Others at Virgin agreed. 'It was great when we arrived,' said Jamie Broadbent, one of the breakfast crew. 'The place had a rock 'n' roll vibe,' he told writer Howard Johnson, who published an unauthorized biography of Chris called *Ginger Nuts* in 2003. 'The staff really wanted us to be there. We were seen as the people who saved them from corporate clutches.'

But after an initial surge in figures, the listeners dropped away and Chris's audience was down 10 per cent after just one year. Disenchanted with being the boss, he sold the station to SMG for £110 million cash, £40 million shares and an agreement that

Scottish Media Group would absorb £75 million of Ginger Productions' debts.

Ginger staff were paid a bonus of a year's salary and Chris announced he would give away much of his own wealth, saying, 'Five million is enough for anyone. I've discussed it with my accountant and, after tax, I'll be able to give away £46 million. To have that amount of money is obscene. No one person needs that much. I'll keep a little for myself, but the rest will go.'

What he actually did was to start buying property, including a townhouse in Chelsea, purchased just after he interviewed Billie and later sold to George Michael for a £500,000 profit. He never lived in it.

Part of the SMG deal stipulated that Chris and his team would continue to present the morning show. But this was not such a successful move. Listening figures had fallen in the face of intense competition from the new BBC Radio 1 breakfast show, presented by Sara Cox (Chris's one-time girlfriend), and the seasoned DJ was now openly bored with his work, regularly missing shows to recover from late nights and blatantly public drinking sessions.

Perhaps this insouciance is why he proposed to Billie that first morning, on air, joking that they could sell the picture rights for the wedding to *OK!* magazine for £1 million and donate the proceeds to charity. Afterwards, he skipped the staff Christmas lunch at celebrity restaurateur Aldo Zilli's West End eatery and took Billie for a private meal.

The next day, and the morning after that, he failed to

turn up at the radio studio. On the Thursday evening, he and Billie were seen in Stringfellows and a succession of clubs and bars, to no one's surprise. But on Friday morning, he did something extraordinary.

When Billie looked out of the window of her apartment in Kilburn, west London, there was a car on the drive. It was a silver Ferrari 360 Modena, festooned with balloons and roses. The keys had been pushed through her letter box with a note. Dazed, Billie opened the door and stared, unaware that Chris was hiding behind a wall to watch her reaction. Billie sat in the driver's seat while a girlfriend fetched a champagne bottle and they toasted the unexpected gift.

'It was the funniest thing you have ever seen,' Chris said to the *Mirror*. 'Her face was classic – I wish I had filmed it. I bought it because life is about having a laugh: it's so important.'

The Ferrari, from Coys of Kensington, could do 189 mph and cost £105,000. 'It's like something out of a film,' Billie said. 'I can't even drive.'

That threw Chris slightly: he hadn't stopped to wonder whether she had a licence. But nothing could spoil his mood and friends who saw him that day said he seemed overjoyed. One long-time associate, Simon Morris, whose happy marriage to his wife Helen had always left Chris feeling envious, was startled when Evans drove up to him on a moped, flipped back his helmet and laughed, 'Si! I've found my Helen!'

A *Mirror* reporter who called to ask why Chris was absent from the breakfast show was told: 'I have bought cars for people before, but never one this expensive. I didn't have anything to do, so I thought I'd buy a car. Billie is ace, a top, top woman. I have high hopes for this relationship. I always do,' he added, self-mockingly. 'We are not an item, but we went out last night and I am seeing her tonight. I don't know what is going on, to be honest, but it is very nice and very enjoyable.'

The tabloids were sceptical. Billie's 'Walk Of Life' single had been released that week and it was due to chart on the Sunday. Conventional record-business wisdom was that this was an elaborate publicity stunt, just as it was widely believed the split with Ritchie had been timed to promote her comeback single, 'Day And Night'.

Conventional wisdom was wrong on all counts. For a start, 'Walk Of Life' flopped, never climbing higher than number twenty-five.

Billie's head was spinning. She told the *News of the World*, 'I'm really flattered. What girl wouldn't be? Chris is rather cute – who knows what's around the corner?'

A day later she was insisting, 'Chris is a lovely guy, but at the end of the day I love Ritch. He's my boyfriend and I want people to know that.'

Ritch didn't know it. He was quick to claim to the *Mirror*'s Anne McClean that he had split up with Billie in November, over his refusal to commit to a long-term relationship. His friends saw it differently. One said, 'Ritchie's gutted about how Chris has gone about things. He'd just got back with Billie after a rocky patch. This is sure to end their relationship once and for all.'

A week after Billie and Chris renewed their acquaintance in this dramatic fashion, Ritchie was arrested at a bar in Dublin's nightlife district with another Five band member, Jason Brown, after a fight broke out. The pair were taken to a police station, charged with public disorder and released on bail three hours later.

On Christmas Day, Billie was in Swindon with her family. Chris was visiting a teenage friend who was seriously ill with cystic fibrosis. When he returned to his home, the Hascombe Court estate near Godalming in Surrey, he called Billie and asked her to come over.

The Pipers were having Christmas dinner. Billie finished her meal and then, with her parents' blessing, booked a car to drive her the ninety miles to Chris's estate. Instead of going to the manor house, they lit the fire in a cottage in the grounds, opened a bottle of wine, pulled the plug out of the TV and talked till dawn.

The next day, Chris told Billie how he felt about her, later explaining to the *Mirror*: 'I just thought, "God, I really, really love you." But I never thought for a second she would feel the same way. Not to such an extent, anyway. I was gobsmacked when she said she did. That was the sealer for me.'

For the run-up to New Year they flew to Funchal, Madeira, where they were almost the only guests at the Savoy Hotel who weren't pensioners. For five days they walked, sunbathed, danced and enjoyed the health spa. The media was instantly intrigued by the budding relationship – one Sunday tabloid went to great lengths to obtain photos of an unmade bed which, they claimed,

With her father, Paul Piper.

With presenter Dani Behr, a fellow graduate of the Sylvia Young Theatre School.

Billie is honoured at *Loaded* magazine's awards ceremony in 2000.

Performing at the *Smash Hits* Poll Winners' Party in December 2000. She didn't know it then, but it was to be one of her last appearances as a pop star.

Bombshell: Billie begins an unexpected relationship with media mogul Chris Evans. Making out in Madeira (*above*); facing the photographers upon their return (*left*).

Leaving Blackfriars Crown Court with her father (*right*), after giving evidence at the 2001 trial of Juliet Peters, who made death threats against Billie and her family.

On holiday with Chris in the Algarve – celebrating their engagement. Billie proposed on April Fool's Day 2001.

Billie the boozer: Mr and Mrs Evans enjoy a celebration drink on their return from Vegas.

Billie in June 2003.

Opposite page: To the happy couple: Billie and Chris wed in Vegas on 6 May 2001. Best man Danny Baker (*back left*) shoots the wedding video.

Billie and Chris at the pub
with Vernon Kay (*above*).
Their honeymoon lasted for over a
year, spanning several continents
and numerous pubs. It was
clouded by a tragic accident: here
the couple attend the funeral of
their friend James Ward (*right*).

proved that Billie and Chris were already sleeping together.

But the couple, as it turned out, had nothing to hide, giving an interview to the *News of the World*'s Mark Nicol to announce their love to the world.

'I've never met anyone like Chris and I love him,' Billie said. 'My dad trusts me completely. He's a Chris Evans fan, but he wanted to talk to him to make sure I was being looked after. They got on great – had a good chat and Dad was just happy for me.'

She firmly explained that Ritchie was history and that she was with Chris now. 'Chris understands me in a way that I don't think any other boyfriend has. And I don't think it's because he is older. We just connected. It really does feel right. I've no idea where all this will end, but we'll take our time, let things develop.'

They hadn't spent a minute apart since Christmas Day. 'Chris is a wonderful free spirit,' Billie said. 'I can honestly say, hand on heart, that this is for real. And it's fun. Chris makes me feel happy and good about myself, and that's all that matters, isn't it? He understands the problems of being in our business but he also understands so much more. And the other wonderful thing about him is that he's happy [for us] to wear matching flip-flops. Not many men would do that, would they?'

The sixteen-year age gap was immaterial, they agreed. Chris said: 'It doesn't bother us in the slightest. She's a lot older and wiser than her years, and I'm a lot younger, so we kind of meet in the middle and it works.'

Years later, she told Piers Morgan: 'I remember my dad washing up with Chris after dinner one night and saying to him suddenly, "Right, what's your game?" I think he felt like he had to say something like that.'

Their affair brought howls of outrage, not least from Ritchie's mum. Kim Dolphin was described by one tabloid as 'stunned': 'I don't know what to think. There is something there which doesn't add up. She is a naive young girl and he is a thirty-four-year-old man. He has gone overboard and he's totally out of order.' Kim, who ran the Crabmill Inn in Bromsgrove, Worcestershire, predicted Billie would be back with her son in the New Year.

And one of Billie's former teachers, David Caldwell of Bradon Forest Secondary, proffered his view: 'I don't think I'm alone in thinking the whole affair quite obscene. She is just a child. I don't know what she can see in him. She probably thinks it's all just a great adventure. It's like watching a mouse on a motorway.'

But many observers, even the professional cynics on newspapers, quickly saw that the emotion between Billie and Chris was real and that both looked happier than they had in a long time. If they didn't understand why Billie needed an older man in her life, maybe they were forgetting that she had lacked the stabilizing influence of her father throughout much of her teens – Paul Piper had four children and he couldn't spend his life following the oldest one around the world, making sure she stayed out of scrapes and offering paternal words of wisdom. Plus, it had been years since Billie had socialized with people her own age, something many commentators didn't realize. She was barely more than a child – but she was living in a very grown-up world.

'Chris Evans was ultimately her saviour,' admits one journalist. 'God knows where she would have ended up if he hadn't stepped in, because there was no one else who was helping her. Her parents probably didn't know what was going on – anyone would assume that if she was surrounded by the people from the record company she was going to be well looked after.

'A lot of people I've interviewed I wouldn't care if I never saw again and I wouldn't dream of approaching them, but Billie was different. I do genuinely care how she is and would like to know that she's happy. It's brilliant to see her doing well. She really deserves it and she's talented. She could have ended up a tortured former child star, but she's got herself together and got back on with it. I can't credit Chris Evans enough, because he got her away from the people who were doing her most harm, at a time when she needed it.'

8 SERIOUS STUFF

Flying back to England after New Year's Eve, Billie steeled herself for a serious statement of emotional intent: she took Chris home to meet her parents. When the plane touched down at Heathrow, she was wearing her new boyfriend's cap, scarf and leather coat – she told friends later that his decision to fly to Madeira, an Atlantic island off the coast of Morocco, had been so sudden that she hadn't had time to go back to her apartment and pack any clothes. They were determined to share everything, even meals – which meant that Chris, a vegetarian, had to eat steak with Billie. 'It was truly horrible,' he said. 'But I just wanted to have the same as her.'

At Hascombe Court they headed straight for the cottage in the grounds, which they had renamed Christmas Cottage. Days were spent walking, drinking in the local pub, cleaning up the cottage, playing board games (Othello was a favourite) and watching *EastEnders* – 'I didn't recognize a soul in it,' Chris said, 'so she had to explain who everyone was for me.'

They told Polly Graham of the *Mirror* they had barely had a cross word since their first date. 'We had one disagreement,' Chris admitted. 'She thinks I should be softer. I am very hard because I have been on my own for so long, and because of what I have achieved. She said I am a bit too hard. There again, I think she is a bit too soft. So if I can get a bit of her sensitivity, and she can get some of my toughness, that will be really good.'

Paul Piper appeared to approve. 'Her dad says as long as she is happy, he is fine,' said Chris. 'And he can see she is happy. He's not the kind of person to give me lectures. I am just as concerned about how I treat her as he is. It's not a problem, because you don't understand how she is so grown-up. If I don't treat her well, she'll just leave. As long as Billie's up for it I am totally up for it. I just hope it lasts the distance, but if she doesn't want to be with me there is nothing I could do about it. I can't force her to stay with me.'

A few days later, he took Billie clothes shopping and the man who could spend £105,000 on a car on a whim was startled to discover that she didn't like to spend money. 'God, I'm a really careful shopper,' she said to the *Star*. 'Something has to be amazing for me to break out in a sweat over it. I'm not a credit-card junkie. I do have a few cards, but I try not to overspend – if I'm feeling sorry for myself and a bit down, I binge in the shops. But if I'm feeling quite sorted, I'm usually happy with what I've got.' She wasn't a label junkie, either, spurning clothes that were overpriced. She found that boring. Instead, she relished hunting for bargains, enjoying the thrill it gave her.

The carefree days were brought to a sharp stop with

the trial of Juliet Peters, the thirty-two-year-old woman accused of sending Billie death threats. Facing five charges of threatening to kill Billie and four of threatening to kill Paul and Mandy Piper, Peters first appeared before a jury at Blackfriars Crown Court in London on Monday 5 February 2001.

The court heard Peters had been in the audience for a taping of Channel Five's *Pepsi Chart Show* in May 2000, where Billie was co-presenter. She had gone to the show because it was free. The video showed that at one moment they had stood side by side. Two weeks later, Peters wrote to her: 'Dear Prima Donna Billie, Why did you give me such a sly, dirty look out of the corner of your eyes before you introduced the break? Who do you think you are? You are a stuck-up, snooty, bitchy, arrogant, spoilt brat. You are still only seventeen. Your parents forced you into the business because they can see the money. Yours angrily, J Peters.'

Letters like that had become run-of-the-mill for Billie, but a series of phone calls took the abuse to a terrifying new level. In the first of several messages left at Innocent's offices in west London, Juliet said: 'Billie Piper, you are a f**king cow and a f**king whore who needs cutting up into little pieces. She is a bitch, she is going to be dead.' Another said, 'Billie Piper's head needs cutting off. She needs decapitating. She needs killing. She needs her body to be set on fire and burnt to cinders where she's banished from our screens so we don't have to suffer her any more.'

In one of thirteen calls to the fan club, she threatened

to decapitate and shoot Billie's parents: 'Billie Piper is a bloody pig and I'm going to kill her parents. I see them out shopping all the time. They are going to get their heads cut off very soon … One bullet through the head should do it.'

Another said: 'She needs her head kicked in and she needs cutting up into little pieces where her head will be in the north of England and her body in the south in a forest somewhere. Next time she appears on stage she's going to be shot dead.'

In the last message, on 25 August, Peters delivered a stream of foul-mouthed invective against Ritchie Neville, calling him 'a gormless f**king four-eyed c**t who wears too much make-up, silly f**king tosser'.

By the time Billie returned from Canada at the beginning of September 2000, police had already arrested Peters at her Canning Town flat. They played Billie the tapes, but partway through the third she broke down in tears and pleaded not to hear any more.

Paul Piper described how his blood had run cold as he listened to Peters address his son, Charlie, by name on one message. 'When I heard his name mentioned it just knocked me for six. He is only a little kid, who likes to play out in the street. It was quite terrifying.'

Talking about the other threats, he said: 'I was disgusted and then I got frightened. These were death threats to my daughter. I can't be with her all the time. I have got to go to work. I was helpless.'

On Tuesday 6 February 2001, Billie arrived at court dressed all in green, with her parents but without Chris

Evans, who told friends he feared he would be a media distraction. She described the tapes as, 'Just awful … It was the worst thing I have ever had to listen to and actually quite scary. I did not know whether to go out or stay in. I was scared about the effect it was going to have on my parents.'

Looking at the jury of five men and seven women, she said, 'I could not understand why anybody would want to say these things. I had done nothing personal and had no intention of upsetting anyone. It was bizarre and it made me cry, and I don't think anyone should have to listen to that.'

She was in the witness box for barely ten minutes, and the strain of it was evident in her voice, which sounded tremulous and close to tears. She told Peters's lawyer, the defence counsel Tom MacKinnon, that she had received poison letters and hate mail from strangers before and that nothing had ever come of the threats, but that the messages Peters had left chilled her in a different way. When she left the court, Billie could not hold back her emotions any longer and clutched her father's hand as she sobbed.

Though Peters denied the charges, she admitted she had made the phone calls – for a laugh. 'I was messing about,' she said. 'I was only joking.'

After leaving school before her sixteenth birthday – like Billie – Peters had drifted, doing menial jobs in fast-food chains before failing at a succession of government training courses. She had been unemployed for ten years and told the court she spent the days sleeping in her flat, watching TV through the night. The calls she made from her home telephone were timed between 3.09 a.m. and 3.47 a.m.

'I didn't intend to harm anyone in any way and I had no intention of someone listening to the answer machine to be taking the threat seriously,' Peters said, telling her lawyer that the claim she had watched the Pipers shopping together was a lie. 'I have never even seen them before in my life.'

The threat to shoot Billie and her parents was a bad joke made after 'the odd whisky or two', she said. 'I would not know where to get a gun from. Even if I did, I could not afford to buy one.'

As the lawyers summed up the evidence, the jury heard conflicting views. Mark Alred, the prosecuting barrister, urged them to remember the fate of John Lennon and George Harrison, attacked by violent fans. Tom MacKinnon said his client was a sad, lonely, solitary person spouting wild gibberish.

Peters was convicted on all nine charges, by a jury that took the unusual step of asking that the defendant be given psychiatric help or counselling. The sentence could have been steep – her crimes carried a maximum penalty of ten years in prison – but after psychiatric reports she was given an eighteen-month suspended sentence and a two-year supervision order, which effectively meant she was free. She had already spent six months on remand at Holloway women's prison.

Issuing a statement for Billie's father, Detective Constable Victoria Merron said: 'He is really proud of his daughter, that she stood up to the threats and had the courage to give evidence. He hopes it will serve as a deterrent to others.'

Billie was determined to put the ordeal behind her. 'This week hasn't been great, it's been quite bad,' she told *The Telegraph*'s Cassandra Jardine, 'but it's been dealt with now. I said my little piece in court and my parents were there with me. It has been horrible for them too. They feel helpless, but they've done the best they can and we've stuck together. It was a shock to the system, but it's over now.'

Days later, she praised Chris, calling him a rock and crediting him, with her parents, for providing the support she had needed to get through the nightmare. 'I felt sick every time I walked into court,' she revealed to the *News of the World*. 'I was really scared, coming face to face with that woman. I couldn't sleep. I was a wreck. I'm very lucky to have people there for me. If I hadn't, God knows what would have happened to me.'

For the first time in a year, she had some time to herself and she decided to use it to do some charity work, promoting the World Vision charity's Orange aPEEL day of fund-raising by schoolchildren to aid youngsters in developing countries. 'It puts things in perspective,' she said. 'Going round hospitals in the UK and seeing these really ill children, and the stress and the bravery and the courage surrounding these people and their families – it makes you appreciate what you do a lot more.'

However, the strain continued to take its toll. A week after the trial ended, Billie collapsed again.

She and Chris had been drinking in the Groucho Club, a favourite meeting place for media people, before moving on to a pub called the Midas Touch. Without warning, she passed out. One drinker at the pub said to the *News of the World*, 'Billie just fell to the ground and was out cold. Chris was great. He quickly helped her to a seat and got her a glass of water. She came back round within seconds and tried to make a joke of it, saying she'd tripped over her handbag. But it was obvious that she hadn't: one minute she was standing up, the next she was on the floor.'

As the scale of their marathon drinking session became clear, fresh fears for Billie's health started to surface. Instead of drug allegations, the emphasis this time was on alcohol: friends reckoned Chris had sunk ten pints of beer and Billie had matched him with halves. For a girl her size to pour five pints of beer on to a recurring kidney ailment seemed to be asking for trouble.

Her PR firm, Vital Publicity, decided this was a crisis too far. Already exasperated with the Chris Evans affair, they announced that all further enquiries should be directed to her record label. 'We feel we got as far as we could go with Billie,' said Dave Pitman. 'We've obviously supported her through a lot of sticky patches.'

Chris reacted by whisking Billie abroad once more. They booked into the five-star Hotel Los Byblos on Spain's Costa del Sol, once a favourite of Princess Diana, and issued no public comment aside from Chris's quip: 'We're on tomato juices.'

Everyone else commented, though. Guests were pestered by reporters for sightings of the couple, who responded by keeping to their room and its private balcony, rarely leaving except to visit the health spa for hot seawater treatments called thalassotherapy. One guest said, 'Chris is really taking care of her, stroking her hair and being as sweet as possible. He obviously realizes how vulnerable and fragile she is, and is being very tender.'

Staff said the couple were sticking to soft drinks, with the odd beer, and taking lots of spa treatments and early nights.

All the usual suspects, including David Price and Ritchie Neville, had their say, and Ritchie's mum Kim was vocal again, accusing Billie of scuppering her pop career by releasing 'Walk Of Life' as a single, in defiance of her record company's wishes. 'Virgin wanted something else to go out, but Billie chose the song, and she had her own way,' said Kim. 'Billie is a very strong-willed girl, but when I see these pictures of her with Chris I wonder how her mum is coping with all this. She's changed completely since she met Chris Evans. She used to be so innocent – now she's totally different. She would have a glass of red wine and that would last the whole evening. She would just sip at it. She was always frightened that if she did get drunk it would get back to her mum. The first thing Billie said she loved about Richard was the fact he didn't drink.'

Amusingly, Ritchie's own boasts about his love of 'getting blotto' were starkly at odds with his mother's puritan claims.

But as Billie and Chris returned to England and got on with being in love, the promised breakdown and split-up didn't happen. Billie hadn't lost the plot, she'd just thrown away the script, and that meant she could wrest control of her life back from the music industry. Her manager, the *Popstars* judge Nicki Chapman, cancelled their contract, letting the press know that her patience had run out and that she blamed Chris Evans.

Billie and Chris were too busy celebrating his thirty-fifth birthday to care. Starting at an Italian restaurant in Notting Hill, they moved on with friends to the Met Bar, which Billie had once professed to hate (perhaps the £300 bottles of champagne they were ordering eased the ordeal for her). Chris managed to make it to the Virgin studios in Golden Square the next day, ninety minutes after his show started, and when Billie joined him they left in a chauffeured limousine for a greasy-spoon cafe: Chris's infallible hangover cure was a fried breakfast. Then they flew to Paris.

The birthday wasn't all they were celebrating. Billie had decided to take the whole summer off. She had told Innocent not to bother releasing her next single, a cover of Blondie's 'The Tide Is High', as scheduled in May, because she wouldn't be promoting it. The rigours of a tour would have meant weeks apart from Chris and she couldn't face that.

Unlike the holidays, this wasn't a spontaneous decision. She'd talked it over carefully with Chris and his friends, discussed it with Mandy and Paul, and she kept coming back to the same fact: nothing about being a pop star was fun any more. That had never been her dream anyway -- as a young pupil at Sylvia Young's theatre school her ultimate ambition had always been to act. When the number ones started to happen, she had imagined her music career would last longer than two years – but then, she hadn't expected the hate mail, the back-stabbing, the drug allegations, the illnesses and the relentless intrusions.

Billie had survived two rides on the rollercoaster and her survival instinct told her not to go back for a third. To many outsiders, though, walking away looked like the stroppiness of a spoilt teen and the only charitable interpretation was that she planned to marry Chris that year. She might even, the gossips whispered, be pregnant. Stoking the rumours, Chris bought a family-sized home in Chelsea for £7.5 million.

Billie didn't deny the marriage stories, simply saying that was a private matter. She told the *News of the World*: 'I love Chris very much and we're just taking things as they come. Since I've been with him I've been on a real health kick. I go jogging every morning and I've started horse-riding because he's bought me one as a present. We just do normal things like any other couple, like going to the pub for a few drinks, watching telly or whatever. Chris is a very caring man and I haven't been happier.'

She was eighteen years old, and about to prove her love in a way she could not have imagined possible when she first walked into Chris's studio just fifteen weeks earlier.

9 VOWS IN VEGAS

Billie proposed in Paris, on April Fool's Day 2001, the day Chris turned thirty-five. He accepted with delight and disbelief and they told friends the wedding would probably happen in August.

Another holiday was called for, to celebrate the engagement, and they flew to the Dona Felipa Hotel in the Vale do Lobo, in the Algarve in Portugal. Though they hadn't exchanged engagement rings, Chris made sure everyone knew they were planning to wed, by letting it slip to reporters after his last radio show before the Easter break.

This holiday was different from the other two intensely romantic getaways. Chris gathered a group of male friends round him for golf and drinking sessions, on one evening sharing a litre of vodka before moving on to pints of lager.

Celebrity-watchers were still not convinced that the relationship was much more than the latest in Chris's series of PR-friendly affairs, pointing to the much-hyped two-week fling with Geri Halliwell. That coincided with a solo single release which took her to number one, but Geri's friends agreed she had believed he loved her and was deeply hurt when it ended. 'She had completely fallen for him,' said one. 'She was so upset and depressed by the whole business she could hardly get out of bed for three weeks.'

Friends of Chris countered that it was Geri's neediness that doomed the affair. He had felt trapped from the moment she moved a fax machine into his bedroom.

His reputation as a womanizer was common knowledge. One member of the production team on *The Big Breakfast*, the show that made him a household name in the early nineties, said to the *Daily Mail*: 'He used to chase girls mercilessly, everyone from guests to the female production team. He just didn't stop. When he suddenly started to hit the big time, I think he regretted being married [to presenter Carol McGiffin] because attractive young girls threw themselves at him. It was hardly a surprise the marriage didn't last. Basically, Chris feels he has something to prove because he is this nerdy-looking guy who knows he wouldn't have had a chance with girls such as Geri Halliwell before he was famous.'

Others gave the couple the benefit of the doubt and tried to fathom the attraction between the teenager and the tycoon almost twice her age. Most agreed that Billie's placid, biddable character was irresistible to Chris, who liked to get his own way in the smallest matters, while she was desperate for a strong, protective man who could tell the rest of the world to get lost.

'Billie is young and naive, which suits Chris perfectly,' a mutual friend explained to the *Daily Mail*. 'He has been involved with a number of strong, intelligent women in the past and if they have dared to question what he says there have been big bust-ups. It's not like that with Billie. Whether she wants to or not, she'll spend all weekend at the pub because she can't bring herself to say no. He has a selfish streak and, really, it's easier to go along with what he wants to save arguments.

'He may believe he's madly in love with Billie. He does have a tendency to think practically every girl he meets is The One. He will certainly enjoy playing teacher to Billie and making her aware of the ways of the world, and she will probably appreciate that. But if he's to make this work, he has some serious growing up to do.'

Others shrewdly pointed out that most of Chris's friends – and he had been surrounded by a loyal core of colleagues and drinking companions for years – were growing up themselves. Many, such as Dan McGrath, one of his breakfast-show posse, were married with small children. They no longer wanted to drink all day and party all night, and they were voluble about the pleasures of parenthood. Chris found it hard to bear the notion that his friends might have something he didn't and he was growing anxious at the thought of becoming middle-aged and lonely.

Back in England, Billie took delight in the kind of teen treats and excursions she'd never had time for before, like a day at a theme park. Chris took her to Chessington World of Adventures in Surrey, where they queued for the Runaway Mine Train and the Dragon

River Ride, and rode the Vampire Rollercoaster, which hurtled so fast that Chris's shoes came off.

And, with the August wedding in mind, she started looking at wedding dresses in Harrods, picking out a £3,000 gown designed by Nottingham-based Catherine Davighi. Woven from silk organza and embroidered with silver and gold thread, it had a boned corset bodice and a full skirt and train, with gold beads at the cuffs. The look was very *Gone with the Wind*, which was why Ms Davighi had called it the Louisiana dress. 'Billie has a fantastic face and the kind of wonderful figure this dress was made for,' said the designer.

Sadly, she didn't get to wear it.

At the beginning of May, Chris asked DJ Harriet Scott to deputize for him on the breakfast slot and told Virgin staff to issue a statement saying he was 'under the weather', while he and Billie flew to Palm Springs, California. They booked into a £200-a-night Moroccan-style self-catering villa at a resort where Winston Churchill once stayed, and ate meals on their balcony or in local restaurants. A waitress who served them said, 'They were all over each other. Their eyes never left each other and they seemed to be in a world of their own.'

A week later, on Saturday 5 May, Chris chartered a private jet from Palm Springs to Las Vegas and the couple took a room at the £175-a-night Harrah's Casino Hotel. A few of his friends, including radio personality Danny Baker and Virgin Radio sports reader John 'Webbo' Webster, flew from Britain without alerting reporters. Even so, at least one tabloid got wind that a Vegas wedding was planned.

They were right. Chris had booked a budget ceremony at the Little Church of the West, where Elvis wed Priscilla and Bob married Paula. Determined to keep the wedding private, he moved the five-minute slot from Sunday lunchtime to the evening.

Instead of the Davighi dress, Billie wore a pink, fringed sarong, a white cropped shirt and pink flip-flops as she stood before Pastor James Hamilton, clutching a bouquet of teardrop roses. Chris was wearing sunglasses, multi-coloured striped trousers and a pale blue shirt with open-toed sandals. The clothes had been bought an hour earlier in a Banana Republic store.

As they took their vows, the organist played 'All I Ask Of You' from *The Phantom of the Opera*, and Wagner's *Lohengrin*. The ceremony was the second cheapest available, at £230, which included Billie's bouquet, Chris's white buttonhole, ten glossy photos and flowers for the church in the price. There were no wedding rings – Chris disliked jewellery.

Four of Chris's friends were there: Webbo, best man Danny Baker, breakfast-show producer Chris Gillett and Gillett's girlfriend, Zana. Mandy and Paul Piper, though, were not present. Billie claimed later that she hadn't warned them what she was doing. 'They would just have told me not to do it. I didn't want to hear any negativity surrounding what I thought was the greatest thing to ever happen to me. I knew they would just have said, "What the hell are you doing?"'

As a result, they probably found out about the wedding when it was reported the next day on Virgin Radio – and for a while they were barely on speaking terms with their daughter.

As they left the chapel, Chris popped a bottle of free champagne and swigged from the neck. 'We've done it,' he declared. 'Isn't it fantastic?' Baker shot the wedding video, filming them as they climbed into a stretch limo to ride back to their hotel. But there were no reporters, no photographers and no comment from the couple or their guests, and only the barest details available from the chapel, built to look like a cowboy-town church. Its owner, Greg Smith, said, 'They looked really happy and had a lovely kiss at the end of the ceremony. They seemed very much in love, to say the least. The only unusual thing was that they didn't exchange rings.'

'It was really romantic,' Billie said. 'But it was so typical of him and me. It was full of personality and that's what any marriage should be.'

Most papers, desperate to report the wedding, were reduced to reciting the litany of other celebrities who had wed at the Little Church: Noel Gallagher and Meg Matthews, Richard Gere and Cindy Crawford, Angelina Jolie and Billy Bob Thornton, as well as Zsa Zsa Gabor, Judy Garland, Mickey Rooney, Telly Savalas, Dudley Moore and Johnny Halliday. None of those partnerships survived, an omen which clearly didn't bother Chris or Billie: unnamed workers at the chapel described them as 'very happy … giggling and laughing all the way through' while afterwards Billie was 'radiant' and Chris was 'grinning like the cat that got the cream'.

A spokesman for Chris's station said: 'Virgin Radio knew of their intention to marry last week but we were sworn to secrecy.' This might have been stretching the truth – some of Chris's friends thought the decision might have been made in Palm Springs. Most agreed Chris had been stressed at the thought of a four-month build-up to a grand wedding at his estate in August, which was what the media were expecting.

'He thought it would be far more romantic just to go off and get hitched,' said one. 'Billie probably would have preferred a more traditional wedding but she is blissfully happy to be Mrs Evans.'

John Webster revealed he'd known about the plans two days earlier, when Chris called him from California and swore him to secrecy. Webster had to pledge not even to tell his own wife, Lisa, or risk getting drunk and spilling the secret to friends. Above all, he had to be on the Sunday morning flight out of Gatwick. A limo was waiting to take him to Chris's hotel at the other end, where the bridegroom was waiting for him by the pool. 'He got out a bottle of champagne and told us they were getting married in an hour. We got changed and went to the chapel. The ceremony was short and sweet,' Webster told Polly Graham in the *Mirror*. 'It was really lovely. They didn't have wedding rings because Chris hates jewellery on men and women. He's got a real thing about it. At first, the [pastor] didn't have a clue who Billie and Chris were, and he was quite abrupt with us when we asked if we could close the door of the chapel to keep out photographers.

'We were all emotional, but there were no tears – it was just a really happy occasion. It was over before we knew it and we drove up and down the strip, drinking champagne in the limo.'

Despite absurd rumours that the party had spent a week in Vegas, running up a £500,000 loss at the tables, Webster revealed they had left the gambling town almost immediately, flying back to Palm Springs on another charter jet and booking into a hotel where, to Webster's horror, he and Danny Baker were assigned the bridal suite: not for the first time, Billie's masculine-sounding name had caused confusion.

'The woman showed us to our room – it was incredible, with a big four-poster bed. I said, "Where's the other bed?" and she said, "Oh, sorry, I thought you were a couple!" Thank God, she took Danny off to another room. I opened the fridge and there were two bottles of champagne and a card saying, "Congratulations on your wedding, Chris and Billie."'

By a bizarre coincidence, almost the first person the newly-weds saw when they arrived back in Britain was Ritchie Neville. He was celebrating a friend's birthday at the Met Bar when the couple walked in. After downing their drinks, they left discreetly. Five split up later that year, and Ritchie's media career fizzled out after a stint on reality-TV show *The Farm*.

Meanwhile Billie was settling into life as a married woman. The discovery that she could wear what she liked, even on her wedding day, was a revelation for her. Instead of a daily wrangle with her wardrobe and the constant chore of fixing her make-up, she could throw on whatever she liked. She could go out with her hair unwashed – other people did. Ordinary people did. And she was ordinary now. She'd worn flip-flops to her budget wedding, and it hadn't mattered: Chris loved her just as much as he would have if she'd worn 200 yards of ivory satin.

Gossip columnists looked at the baggy sweatshirts and jogging bottoms and speculated that she must be hiding a pregnancy. Ian Hyland in the *Sunday Mirror* tutted: 'As she snuggled up to Chris in a pub in Knightsbridge, she appeared to have forgotten how to use a comb.'

It was this scruffiness – not the romance with a millionaire, not the sixteen-year age gap and not the secret wedding – which prompted Mandy Piper to give only the second full interview of her daughter's career. Opening her heart to Nadia Cohen of the *Daily Mail*, Mandy said: 'Billie and Chris seem to have become a scruffier version of Posh and Becks. She used to get very upset when there were pictures of her in the paper making her look fat or in a mess – she is now beyond caring.'

Mandy said she and Paul had not been barred from the wedding, despite what some of the more vicious rumours claimed. They had simply not been able to drop all their responsibilities and fly to the Nevada desert in time for the ceremony, with only a day or two's notice. Billie, after all, had a brother and two sisters, all of them at school. And the wedding had taken place during term-time. Though they were disappointed not to be there for the big day, Mandy stressed that she and Paul knew about the planned ceremony and hadn't been kept in the dark. Billie and Chris's desire to wed quickly simply meant that the family was unable to attend: there had been too much to sort out in too short a space of time. She was thrilled for her daughter, though: 'I am just happy because Billie is happy.'

As well as giving her happiness, marriage to Chris seemed to have calmed Billie. Gone were the highly-strung days of not knowing what time or date it was; gone was the never-ending pressure to succeed. In Mandy's view, marrying Chris gave Billie a chance to relax, to take time out and gain a new perspective on her life, achievements and career.

The Pipers clearly liked their new son-in-law. A bit wild he might be, but he was also a survivor, a wealthy man with a lot of experience in the back-stabbing world of the media, who could protect Billie from people seeking to exploit her or lead her into danger. 'I definitely feel she is safer under Chris's wing,' confided Mandy. Her eternal worries from Billie's younger days, when she fretted about her under-age daughter's party-loving lifestyle, were soothed by the thought that Billie now had a solicitous escort in the clubs and pubs of London.

And there was another change in Billie, too. The erstwhile stage-school student, born with a passion for performance, had never been concerned with sports before. But as her new husband was a keen fan, Billie now found herself following Chris's interests with enthusiasm. Golf, football, cricket – Billie was learning fast, and even went to Lord's with her man. Her mother, well aware of Billie's former disinterest, was touched to see this change in her daughter, feeling it proved how deeply she felt about Chris.

Hinting that Billie had already started to think about switching her career to acting, Mandy admitted that they had talked about her plans for the future, but refused to reveal exactly what they were. 'I know what she is going to do next, but she'll kill me if I tell you any more.' She hinted strongly, however, that it would perhaps lie outside of the music industry.

Looking to the future in a different way, although the possibility of grandchildren was inevitably something she'd discussed with her daughter, Mandy was not eager to fuel speculation that Billie could already be pregnant. Her only comment on the matter was that Billie was still of an age when starting a family would be a little premature.

It was a controlled performance, proving she had learned a lesson from her disastrous 'sex-and-drugs-and-anorexia' interview a year earlier. Yet raw emotion shone through too: 'The truth is we don't see much of her any more now she is with Chris.' But she was pragmatic, reflecting that this was the eternal plight of parents: when things are going well, children are happily inattentive to their folks. It's only when there are difficulties that a mother's advice is sought.

Luckily for Mandy, those dark days of worrying about her daughter going off the rails seemed to be contained within the past now. She confessed that every time she'd read another story about Billie being out on the town, or collapsing in a bar, she was terribly anxious. She barely saw her daughter once her music career became stratospheric, what with Billie jet-setting around the world on exhausting promotional tours and living on her own in London. While concerned – even to this day – that Billie perhaps lost a chunk of her childhood because of her success, Mandy was now able to put the tabloid scare-stories into perspective, reflecting that Billie was simply living out her teen years as every adolescent does. And she wouldn't change things for the world, saying proudly: 'At least she has done something with her life and can look back and say she has achieved something.'

Secretly, however, despite her delight in Billie's runaway success, Mandy hoped that her rollercoaster life might now be coming to a quiet period. Billie had been high-profile for the most important and formative years of her life, and Mandy felt that her daughter deserved some time away from the spotlight. But she conceded, 'Of course now she is married to Chris, there is no chance of that.'

But on that last point, Mandy needn't have been so concerned.

10 A HUNDRED DAYS' HOLIDAY

Virgin sacked Chris Evans at the end of June 2001, after he failed to turn up at work for six days in a row. He had told his bosses he was too unwell to be on the air, but he was seen with Billie and their friends in bars, pubs and off-licences all over London on a marathon drinking session. 'Unwell as a newt,' commented *The Sunday Times*.

His breakfast show was in the doldrums, despite his efforts to revamp the format. While his rival, former girlfriend Sara Cox on Radio 1, drew 7 million listeners daily, Chris's programme had an audience of just 1.75 million. This looked like the end of the most unconventional career in broadcasting.

The problem was, after running the station for two years, Chris could not reignite his enthusiasm for being an employee. The succession of holidays with Billie and the series of days off for sickness now pushed SMG's patience to the limit. When he cried off the show after a night of drinking with Aldo Zilli, he was burning his last bridge. Badly hung-over, he walked with Billie to their local pub in Belgravia in the middle of the morning and ordered a lager. He followed that with cider, Bloody Marys and whiskies with water, while Billie had three vodkas with Red Bull before switching to lemonade. When their cash ran out, they started a tab.

Tabloid news editors quickly heard he was there, instead of on his sickbed, and sent photographers. Rumours started that he and Billie had been rowing furiously, but John Webster, who had met Chris as a cameraman on his golf show *Tee Time*, insists that was nonsense. 'I turned up at the pub about ten minutes after it was supposed to have happened,' he told Polly Graham of the *Mirror*, 'and Billie was there and seemed fine. She didn't look like she'd been crying and didn't even mention it. She was happy as pie.'

The session went on for six days, with Billie and Chris appearing on the front pages with a supermarket trolley laden with cans and bottles. On 28 June, SMG announced they had no option but to terminate his contract. Chris and Billie responded by going on holiday.

Within two weeks, Billie had decided for certain that she didn't want to go back to making pop music. Innocent Records had shut down her web site, but they still expected a third album from her – their usual response, when pestered to comment on what was going on in Billie's life, was that she was 'working on new songs'.

Chris's agent, Michael Foster at ARG, had taken her under his wing and contacted Hugh Goldsmith to say she wouldn't be going back to the studio. Innocent couldn't quite believe it. A year before, she'd been a chart-topper: she must want to revive that success. And surely this marriage to the most famous unemployed man in Britain couldn't hold back her career for long.

Goldsmith agreed to shelve the third album until Billie was ready to honour her commitments, but emphasized to Foster that Virgin had invested a huge amount of money in launching and promoting her. Bailing out wasn't supposed to be an option.

Billie did not issue an official statement, but friends were briefed to tell her side of the story. 'Billie has had enough,' said one to the *Daily Mail*. 'She has given her pound of flesh to the record people. She has told Virgin that they have had the benefit of her "growing-up" years, and she doesn't want to give them any more. She wants to move on. She is retiring as a pop star.'

She had always known the music business wouldn't sustain her for ever, and she'd been frank about it to interviewers. When pop journalists wanted to know if she saw herself at number one in ten years' time, she always underlined her other ambitions. 'When I get to about twenty-five I can say, "Well, I've done the pop star thing,"' she told one magazine. 'Then I'll become an actress for a while, and then I'll have my own business. Then I can spend the rest of my life chilling out.' To another reporter, she said she planned to be running her own record company by the time she was forty-five, after a successful career in movies. Lots of teenagers have those confident dreams, but she was the only one who could tick the first box: 'Become an international star at fifteen.'

Celeb-watchers wrung their hands and implied that Billie's effervescent personality had been blown apart by Chris Evans's rampant ego, like a tank shell hitting a helium balloon. *The Guardian*'s Caroline Sullivan said: 'Like every eighteen-year-old who has ever lived, Billie probably thinks she knows it all, when in fact she has got herself into a fix that a grown woman would do her utmost to avoid.' Mark Jagasia, showbiz correspondent at the *Express*, said Chris Evans was 'an overbearing character, and she reacts by trying to keep up with his binges. But she's no match for him'.

Friends knew better. 'People have accused Chris of manipulating Billie, but that's just not true. [They] are right for each other,' said John Webster to the *Mirror*. 'She has been a very calming influence on him. She is remarkably level-headed and mature. They both wear the trousers in that household. She goes out with her friends and Chris goes out with his.'

Webster also denied the other rumour which was rife – that Billie was expecting a baby. 'I don't think it will be for a while,' he said. 'Billie is definitely not pregnant.'

She was ready to draw a line under her pop career – but that didn't mean she had to embrace motherhood at eighteen.

For the first time since she was fifteen, Billie had a normal birthday when she turned nineteen. No cakes from tabloid newspapers, no sniffer dogs outside the club, no inebriated stars from boy bands and girl groups, no paparazzi, no cars from record companies, no snide asides in the gossip pages the next day.

Instead, Chris and Billie were taking it easy in Los Angeles, staying at the Sunset Marquis, looking at properties in the Hollywood Hills and eating in restaurants on Sunset Strip.

The jaunt had begun in July and became one of the longest and most idyllic honeymoons on record. They took a break on the Isle of Wight – where, a year later, a tragedy was to mark the end of the honeymoon – and then flew to Disney World in Florida, with best man Danny Baker and his family.

They told friends they were taking a hundred days' holiday. By the time that was coming to an end, around November, they had decided to award themselves another hundred. It didn't take a psychologist to wonder if 'holiday' was a euphemism for 'running away'.

'The moment I walked away was the moment I started to get better,' Chris commented years later to *The Mail on Sunday*. 'It was instantaneous. Getting out of that mad, intense whirl was the only thing I could do to stay sane. I was desperate. Absolutely desperate. People think that having that lifestyle and being that famous is amazing, but I was so totally unhappy. I was out all the time, surrounded by all these people, doing whatever I wanted. But I remember looking at all these friends around me and realizing that most of them were on my payroll.

'The problem was that I was actually a pretty normal bloke, and because of that I had no idea how to handle things. It's not good to get everything you want. In fact, it's pretty horrible. I didn't need a psychiatrist to tell me what was wrong with me and I didn't need anyone to tell me what to do about it. It just got to the point where I knew I had to get off the ride, stop everything and walk away. That's what I did. I couldn't think about the fact that I had all these people on my payroll, I couldn't think about the fact I had commissions. I just had to get out. So I shut up shop and just left.'

After a romantic weekend in Southwold, on the Suffolk coast, Billie and Chris spent the festive season at Christmas Cottage, where they had fallen in love, and raised money for local charities by selling Christmas trees in the pub car park. Locals were used to their antics by now and barely glanced twice at the chart-topper and her millionaire husband, Santa Claus hats pulled down over their ears, jumping on the spot and hugging each other to keep the cold at bay.

Portugal's Algarve had proved a perfect hideaway in the spring, so they returned … but this time to buy. They chose a pair of villas in Quinta do Lago, where ex-England striker Alan Shearer also had a holiday home and Chris's Uncle Brian was director of the nearby Pinheiros Altos Golf Club. It wasn't the only place to play golf – and there were plenty of bars catering for Brits abroad, including the Melting Pot, the Pig and Whistle and Rumours, in Almancil down the road.

'They're having a wonderful time,' said one friend, adding that neither of them had any plans to get back to work. 'Chris is very much enjoying life out there, playing golf and entertaining friends. I don't think he's even thought about when he and Billie will come back yet. The thing is, they're both having a really good time.'

They weren't living in the villas: instead, they had rented a nearby property and hired a brigade of builders to convert the two properties into one. The smaller house was to be offices and a recording studio, connected by a covered walkway to the main building, where seven bedrooms gave them ample living space. The property was set in two acres of landscaped gardens, including a swimming pool, and had set them back £2.5 million; the conversion was costing another million.

Billie was entranced by Portugal. She spent her days exploring the hills in her olive-green Jaguar sports car with its soft top, which she kept down even in the rain (yes; the most famous non-driver in the world had finally learned to drive). Chris drove a gold Range Rover, though rarely further than the golf course.

They cut down on their drinking sessions, just opening a bottle of wine in the evenings while they stayed indoors and watched videos. And they made no effort to hide their happiness. 'I've never seen Chris so contented,' remarked Webster to the *News of the World*. 'You know the phrase "happy as Larry"? Well, Chris makes Larry look like a miserable git. They're the kind of couple who can do nothing for days on end and still be happy. They watch videos for hours. They both adore *The Sopranos* and watch it again and again.'

There was only one speck on their horizon: Billie didn't want children yet and Chris was keen to start a family. He was confident he could persuade her, though: 'They will definitely have kids together very soon,' said 'Webbo'. 'Chris told me they want them; that's all part and parcel of their happiness.'

Few of the old gang were in touch with them. Relations with other stars of the breakfast crew were strained, because of the way it had fallen apart. But Danny Baker called regularly. 'I still speak to Chris all the time,' he said. 'He's very, very happy. He's just living life for pleasure. Nothing wrong with that.'

Billie was almost invisible. The press assumed she had been swallowed up by Chris's ego, but their friends understood she was an equal partner in the marriage. 'All Chris really likes to talk about these days is him and Billie,' said one. 'They're still really, really in love. If you see them together, you can tell that they are completely wrapped up in each other.'

Even their choice of videos was about more than just entertainment. Chris wanted Billie to understand everything about him, even what he'd laughed at as a child, so they stocked up on old episodes of *Morecambe and Wise* and *Monty Python*.

Domestic life became even cosier when Paul and Mandy moved to Spain's Costa del Sol. They had sold Billie's childhood home in Swindon for £250,000 before Christmas and originally thought of moving to the south coast, perhaps Bournemouth. Chris was eager to be a popular son-in-law and offered to help out financially. The thought of how good life could be beside the Med instead of the English Channel was tempting, and the knowledge that Quinta do Lago was only a few hours' drive away clinched it.

The Pipers bought a £350,000 villa near Fuengirola, between Malaga and Marbella. Perched on a wooded hillside in an acre of grounds, it had a twenty-metre swimming pool and made the ideal base for the children's new life abroad: Charlie was twelve, Harley eleven and Ellie nine.

'It's nice to have Billie so near,' said Mandy to *The Sun*, adding that she saw her daughter several times soon after the move. 'She's only a stone's throw away. They are very happy with life. Good luck to them – I can understand why they wouldn't want to return to England. We certainly don't plan to. I just wish we had done this a long time ago. We didn't because of Billie and her career and the other kids, but now she is with Chris and happily married we felt we could give it a go.'

Mandy hinted again that when Billie returned to showbiz, she would want to act, not sing. She revealed to the *Daily Mail*: 'Since the wedding she seems so much more settled. She's under less pressure and can finally sit back and look at things in perspective. It was all so fraught for her over the last few years, with all the endless record promotions. The way record companies market and promote these youngsters is very tough, pushing them into the limelight. Half of these young stars – and Billie was far from the only one – don't even know what time of day it is. I can remember Billie ringing me to ask what day of the week it was. She was not happy for quite a long time, but now she definitely is, which is great.'

On trips back to Surrey, Billie and Chris enjoyed a few pints at the White Horse in the village of Hascombe. 'Chris loves a pint of Adnam's ale and complained he couldn't get it abroad,' said James Ward, who ran the White Horse with his partner, Sue Barnett. 'He and Billie like having lunch here. They know they can be left in peace if they want.'

And not only lunch: Chris sometimes took Billie for breakfast at the pub, even though the doors were locked and the landlord asleep upstairs. They would climb through a window at the back, pour a drink and settle in, chatting about the wrought-iron gates they planned to hang at the entrance to the estate, the landscaping work they were doing in the grounds or their efforts to get a village cricket team together.

As their first wedding anniversary rolled around, they were back in America, Billie never photographed in anything but baggy tracksuits and flip-flops, with her unkempt hair crammed under a flat cloth cap. Chris called her his 'pretty little scruff'. They were in Los Angeles because they owned a Hollywood house, with Brad Pitt, Jennifer Aniston and Leo DiCaprio for neighbours. The £5.6-million mansion had once been owned by Lionel Richie. But really they were there because Chris decided that was where they were going, and Billie was content to let him make the decisions. 'She's happy to go wherever he wants to go and do whatever he wants to do,' said a friend to the *Daily Mail*. 'He absolutely adores her. She's the perfect companion for him: easy-going and totally undemanding.'

Most days started with a late breakfast at a diner, before trawling through the furniture stores for anything that would look good in their new home. They didn't shop the Michael Jackson way, buying stock as fast as they could point to it, but the Billie way: browsing for hours, weighing up prices and choosing only what they fell in love with ... such as a pair of matching 'his and hers' Ford Mustangs for $60,000.

Billie commended her husband on his shopping technique, revealing that he was a great person to share a spot of retail therapy with. Not only encouraging with his compliments (and, presumably, his wallet), he was also hands-on in hunting out bargains, accessories and the right sizes in each.

Record shops and classic-car auctions drew them and they enjoyed bowling at the alleys, but were rarely out after dark. A fan who spotted them at a Celine Dion concert commented, 'They were very lovey-dovey indeed.'

A friend said: 'They are making a different kind of life in America, away from the media glare. Los Angeles is a much more open and relaxed environment. That's what Chris and Billie want at the moment. They want some time out.'

The biggest problem was nothing to do with the relationship. The mansion had rats. Exterminators were called in to set traps all over the five-bedroom, 6,000-square-foot property and they returned at least six times during May to make certain the rodents were gone. 'It isn't every day you have rats in such an expensive house,' commented a worker with the Western Exterminator Company. 'I'm sure Mr Evans didn't expect his home to be infested after spending so much money on the place.'

They didn't come back to England until August 2002. Ready to restart their careers, but feeling the effects of a year-long holiday, they booked into a health farm for three days. Grayshott Hall in Surrey was ten miles from the estate at Hascombe – far enough to quell the temptation for a swift pint at the White Horse. The £200-a-night spa, in a country house once owned by the Poet Laureate Lord Tennyson, warned guests: 'Please be aware that alcohol is not available in the interests of your total health and recuperation.' As compensation, it offered a gym, tennis courts, a pool, a golf course, badminton, croquet, a sauna and a steam room. Past guests included Monica Lewinsky, the Duchess of York, Dale Winton and Emma Thompson.

Everything seemed ideal. Then tragedy struck.

11 CLOUDS ON THE HORIZON

James Ward, landlord of the White Horse, kept a yacht called *Nausicaa* on the coast in Hampshire. On Wednesday 7 August 2002, to celebrate his partner Sue Barnett's fifty-fifth birthday, he sailed across the Solent to Cowes on the Isle of Wight with a party of friends, including Chris and John Webster. Billie didn't join them.

The harbour was crowded, as boats swarmed in for the annual regatta, and the party pushed on to nearby Yarmouth, where they had a few drinks at the George Hotel before eating at Salty's restaurant. It was one of Chris's favourite haunts: he'd taken Billie there the summer before. James introduced Chris to a friend, Peter Molleson, who said later: 'He was drinking but was not drunk, and the skipper was definitely not inebriated. He was very convivial, but not drinking as much as the rest of the party. It was quite a shindig, quite a wild night – this is normal for Salty's.'

Chris, James and the group left at 6.30 p.m., before the evening really got underway. There were still a couple of hours of daylight and they steered a course for Hamble, where James kept the 31-foot yacht. As there

was a gentle breeze, *Nausicaa* was running under sail as
well as her engine.

Just before 9.15 p.m., as the sails were coming down,
the boom, a heavy crosspiece that secures the base of a
yacht's triangular sail, swung round. It struck James,
knocking him overboard. When he hit the water he was
unconscious. Like the others on board, he wasn't
wearing a life jacket.

Panic gripped the party. James was the only experienced sailor among them, the only one who could even
operate the VHF radio. They didn't know how to sail
the boat or call for help. According to Sue's father, Des
Smith, who learned of the accident from his daughter,
the inexperienced crew tried to halt the yacht and turn
it round, but by the time they had managed to change
course they had lost sight of James's body. One of them
dived overboard in a desperate rescue attempt, but the
sky was getting dark and the water was rough and icy
cold, and he was quickly in difficulties.

One of the party pulled out a mobile phone and
dialled 999 and coastguards alerted a police launch. A
helicopter was sent and other boats on the water, off the
Brambles Bank, about a mile and a half from the Isle of
Wight, tried to help.

Lifeguard Justin Bloomfield told newspapers he had
dived into the water in a last-ditch attempt to save the
drowning man, after hearing the coastguard's appeal
for help and racing across the Solent from Cowes in a
rigid inflatable boat. He spotted the *Nausicaa* by its
navigation lights, because the crew didn't know how to

operate any of the other beams that might have made it easier to see. 'We spotted a lifebelt,' said Bloomfield, 'that the crew had obviously thrown overboard to help their skipper. The light on it was flashing so we left it as a marker. We saw the body just a few metres away. It was floating upside down and looked lifeless. I swam to the body. He felt bitterly cold.

'The water was freezing and quite choppy, but I turned the man on his back and tried to open his airways and keep his head above the waves. My first thought was that he was dead. He was just wearing a T-shirt and shorts. I put him across my body and supported him. I pulled a muscle in my groin, swimming against the tide. At that point a lifeboat turned up and took him. They tried to resuscitate him, but it was obvious he was dead. I could see the *Nausicaa* in the distance and hear the crew shouting, but I couldn't make out what they were saying. They sounded absolutely terrified and clearly panicking.'

Police confirmed James's death had nothing to do with alcohol: it was an accident that could happen to even the most experienced sailor, said PC Stuart Revelle of the Southampton Police Marine Unit. 'I went on board the vessel and everyone was dazed,' he said. 'There were personal recriminations, with one man saying, "What did I do wrong?" They were all going through what had happened.

'One man had jumped in to try to make a rescue, which was very risky. But I think there was nothing he could have done. I didn't see any evidence that there had been a great deal of drinking. In my opinion, drink was not a factor. They were totally coherent. Some were very quiet while others were over-the-top noisy. Chris Evans didn't say a word. He was traumatized and very upset.'

Mark Clark, of the Maritime and Coastguard Agency, had harsh words for the party, saying they had not adhered to safety recommendations. 'The crew appeared to be ignorant of what to do in an emergency and it was fortunate that they were in a mobile-signal area. They were unfamiliar with the layout of the cockpit and unfamiliar with the radio. It was almost dark when they contacted us and they were not even able to switch on the lights so that we could direct an Isle of Wight ferry that was in the area.'

Billie helped her husband to arrange the funeral, but she found it difficult to relate to what he had been through. She had no experience of supporting people after a trauma and all her life she had dealt with bad things by refusing to dwell on them. The tragedy opened wounds beneath the surface of their relationship, scars that they couldn't see at first. When the landlord of their local inn drowned, something in Billie's marriage died too.

However, she was still only nineteen years old and, despite the accident, she needed to move forward in her life. At an age when most people are starting to think about starting a career, she was ready for her second one.

Hugh Goldsmith was eager for her to start recording a third album and she did meet with songwriters, but her real ambition was to start acting. 'That's what I'm gonna do,' she told friends. 'Acting, acting, acting!' And unlike her pop stardom, that wasn't going to happen overnight. So she threw herself into auditions and Chris began a manic round of meetings and ideas sessions as he prepared to launch a variety of pilot shows on Channel 4 and Channel Five.

Billie worked hard to convince theatre and film directors that she was right for their shows. Her first intention was to act on TV and when a role in a major drama came up she auditioned confidently. She didn't get it, though at first it looked like the part was hers. When the call came to tell her she'd missed out, for a few hours Billie was knocked back, shocked; all through her career, she'd been used to getting it right first time.

She bounced straight back. The disappointment didn't even last a day. There were other roles, other auditions, and she'd keep scrapping till she broke through.

Noel Coward's *Hay Fever* was being revived in the West End and for a time it seemed she would make a prestigious theatre debut. When that didn't come off, she switched tactics and joined Chris in negotiations for the launch of *Popstars: The Rivals*. He would be a judge, she'd be the presenter and choreographer, but the project fell through when Chris couldn't secure a deal for a share of the profits.

Her first break, when it came, was not so big. Working Title Films, the British movie company behind *Four Weddings and a Funeral* and *Bridget Jones's Diary*, was shooting a low-budget comedy called *The Calcium Kid*, a mockumentary about a milkman-turned-boxer. Orlando Bloom, who played Legolas in *The Lord of the Rings*, was Jimmy, the hero, and Billie was his love interest, Angel. It was a small role, in a low-key movie. It took only a few days to shoot Billie's lines. But it was a start.

Chris and Billie spent Christmas abroad for the first time. With Billie's parents in Spain and the White Horse too full of sad memories, it seemed hollow to hole up in Christmas Cottage again. So they flew to Barbados and lounged on the beach at the Sandy Lane Hotel, reading and sipping cocktails.

Billie and Chris had lived by two simple rules throughout their marriage: don't bring home worries from work and never argue after drinking. Since they had spent more than a year without working and almost every day involved a few drinks, it was the perfect formula.

But since the drowning, Chris had been more short-tempered, whether he was drinking or not. He'd always been belligerent – his ex-wife Carol McGiffin said he could pick a fight with Mother Teresa – but now he couldn't seem to plug into Billie's easy-going, calming influence.

After a week of convivial living at the Sandy Lane, Chris got into a steaming row with a barman. The dispute was petty, over charges for a round of drinks that Chris couldn't remember ordering. As Chris's voice rose and guests started to stare, Billie suggested they should just pay the bill and forget it: with rooms at £2,100 a night, was a £50 bar tab worth the hassle?

Chris refused. With the dispute suddenly threatening to wreck the day, Billie asserted herself. 'Let's not do this any more,' she said, and paid the whole bill.

According to guests who watched in open-mouthed embarrassment, Chris 'went ballistic'. He accused her of undermining him and shouted until Billie burst into tears and walked out. A barman asked Chris to leave a few moments later. The following day they spent apart, with Billie joining friends on a yacht.

They were together and smiling for a public appearance in February 2003, at a fund-raising gala at the Old Vic. Chris had shaved off the bushy beard that had made him look like Robinson Crusoe on the Barbados beaches and they chatted with Dame Judi Dench, who advised Billie to keep auditioning for roles. Back at Hascombe, they bought a pair of lurchers, Epstein and Percy, and took the dogs on long tramps along the lanes.

Later in the month they were property-hunting again, this time in Ireland. Chris was drawn to the remote Mourne Mountains of County Down, where they could go walking or sailing. He was gripped by a need to 'hang out in peace, getting away from it all, having some fun and relaxing', said a friend to the *Sunday Mirror*. Whether Northern Ireland was the ideal base to relaunch Billie's career, the friend didn't say.

Rumours were spreading that Billie and Chris were no longer the idyllic couple. They wanted different things. For more than a year, Chris had wanted what Chris wanted and Billie had wanted that too, whether it was getting married in flip-flops or watching classic comedies in a half-converted Portuguese villa.

The change in Billie was not instantly obvious. Friends still talked of the happiest couple in show business: 'The relationship works because Billie is incredibly easy-going,' said one. 'They rarely spend more than a few hours apart. They stay in together almost every night. Chris always decides.'

Kevin Lygo, director of programmes at Channel Five and a long-time friend of Chris, confirmed: 'Billie is a really good influence on his life. He is as settled and as happy as I have ever known him. I think that the year off and Billie's presence have helped him to solve the problem of what to do with your life if you have £50 million.'

The rumours of a split were being spread maliciously, said Chris's spokesman, Matthew Freud of Freud Communications, and they might not be unconnected with the court case between Chris and Virgin Radio over his dismissal.

After eight months on the job market, Billie's chance came. She was cast in an adaptation of 'The Miller's Tale' opposite Dennis Waterman, one of a series of BBC versions of Chaucer's *Canterbury Tales*. She finally had the opportunity to prove her talent and she seized it hungrily. To signal she was back in the spotlight, she agreed to do a magazine cover shoot for *Marie Claire*, in a £6,000 toga designed by Julien Macdonald and festooned with hand-stitched Swarovski crystals. The magazine featured four different covers: the other stars were Cat Deeley, Denise Van Outen and Martine McCutcheon, all of them supporting different charities. Billie's was Rape Crisis.

Filming *The Miller's Tale* was a joy. For a start, she was starring with Waterman and James Nesbitt – 'two actors who could not give a bad performance at gunpoint', said *The Mail on Sunday*'s critic. But the best thing was to be giving a real performance, for a grown-up audience. Every day she arrived on set to be the queen of karaoke at Waterman's pub, sending up her pop diva image and playing every song for laughs.

Meanwhile, Chris's court battle was coming to a nasty climax. In a caustic summing-up, the High Court judge Mr Justice Lightman said: 'Despite his confident front, [Chris Evans] is very insecure in himself … Others who know him and want any continuing future relationship with him must … avoid any confrontation or cause for upsetting him …

'To achieve what he wants without confrontation, he is manipulative and has to resort to any means, fair or foul, to achieve his ends. His success and character [make him] accustomed to and insistent on getting his own way … He is petulant and given to sulking and walking away from situations whenever he considers himself thwarted. He is not ready to make concessions to others. He is a person who cannot tolerate either criticism or the exercise by management of authority over what he does.

'He has the temperament of a prima donna. He always expects and demands compliance with his wishes. He has a low "tolerance" threshold and he has a marked propensity displayed throughout his career of "walking out" on his contractual commitments when (as he perceives it) the going gets hard.'

Unsurprisingly, he lost the case. Worse still, it cost him £7 million.

Billie didn't know how to talk to her husband about what he was going through. 'If he came home and I said, "Oh my God, I'm so sorry about your loss," he'd be like, "Put the kettle on." Stress and money – that kind of stuff can kill people. You have to make a conscious effort to switch off because it's just not important,' she said to the *Evening Standard*.

So Billie and Chris did what they always did and went on holiday, this time to the St Jean Cap Ferrat in the South of France, for a five-day stay at the Voile d'Or Hotel. The difference was that this time, when they came home, Billie was ready to start talking to the press.

Officially, the interviews were to publicize *The Miller's Tale*, which was scheduled to go out at 9 p.m. on 11 September 2003. But the real question, phrased twenty different ways, focused on her marriage: 'What's that all about then?'

Billie was happy to discuss it. In a series of interviews, she laid bare her emotions, her ambitions, her relationships and her insecurities. For the first time, she had no PR minder at her side, fending off difficult questions or slipping her scripted answers. And more importantly, she had an intense desire to talk about her life. She'd been silent for too long. She was about to make up for it.

12 SPEAKING OUT

'It was a bit like Little Red Riding Hood and the Big Bad Wolf' – that was how Billie described the way a man twice her age made her fall in love with him. 'But I liked that. I found it sexy. I don't care what anybody else said, the whole thing was sexy.'

Red Riding Hood wanted to be caught. She made that plain in every interview. Even before she hugged him in the Virgin studio, Billie fancied Chris – and she'd heard that he liked her too. For days before they met, she'd been thinking about what might happen. 'I could understand why he only had beautiful girlfriends,' she told Simon Cage of *New Woman* magazine.

'When we first met [he said] he wanted to marry me and we'd do it for charity, but being a girl I didn't take it light-heartedly. I kind of went, "Yeah, ha, ha … Ohhh … He wants to marry me! He said it!" I did think about it straight away.'

The Ferrari on her drive, dripping with roses, after their first date, won her heart: 'I thought, "I'm gonna marry that guy." Not because of what it was, but because I thought, "I wanna get to know somebody that does something like that." It's a huge statement. The way it stopped me in my tracks, I loved that. I love people that are straight down the line and I hate all that mind-game bollocks. I need to know or go, because I can't hang around waiting for answers.'

Chris wasn't the kind to keep her hanging around. She got the answer she needed to hear on Christmas Day. The moment she got there, he kissed her. There was to be none of that 'He-loves-me-he-loves-me-not' confusion. And Billie was just as keen. 'I really fancied him. He's so charming and so engaging, you never know what he's going to do. It was perfect. What we had was so right and was so going to work because we really wanted it, both of us. It was instant and those things very rarely happen, so you can't just let them go and you can't think about it and weigh things up. You've just got to go with it.'

She claimed she didn't even tell Mandy and Paul she was getting married until after the ceremony, and added that she'd never asked them what they thought about their daughter marrying a man only a few years younger than they were. That didn't tally with what Chris and her parents had been saying a couple of years earlier, but it did underline her message: no regrets.

'I was just being a bit selfish at the time. I didn't care about anybody else, which can be a bit dangerous but I've got really close friends and I knew that they'd forgive me if I just took off. It was just for us, not anybody else.'

She didn't feel she'd missed out on a white wedding, emphasizing that the most important thing for her and

Chris was that it was their day. That was all that mattered. Not only did they bypass the family traumas weddings can generate, but they had none of the organizational headaches either. All they wanted was a fun day that celebrated their love – and that's what they got.

Listing Chris's best qualities, Billie would talk about his sense of humour, his readiness to take a risk and his tireless energy. 'He has this ability to bring out the best in everybody,' she told *The Guardian*'s Emma Brockes. 'When we're out together we are like a double act. He'll always be a party boy and I'll always be a party girl. We're very rarely in bad moods. There's no reason for us to be. If everybody was as lucky as us, they'd rarely fight.'

She had needed Chris's love and his stabilizing influence to make her see how lucky she was, though. When they met, she had felt trapped and she was desperate to get off the treadmill. She acknowledged, now, just how exhausted she had been. That blinkered pursuit of success – drama school, the *Smash Hits* ad and then a fully-fledged career as a pop star – had taken its toll. For Billie, it had been time for a quiet life. 'I just needed to do some normal things and not worry about the consequences: eat some curries. Stay in bed for a whole day. Go and watch movies back to back for three days. Treat myself to some Häagen-Dazs. I missed life! Because being a pop star and being a film star is not real. It's a job.'

She had loved it at first, though. 'I was so starry-eyed. I just couldn't wait to get to bed and get back up again. And I was so ambitious. But it became a bit lonely when I travelled. It's a sad existence … It was fun, it was a really good time, but I'd had enough by the end of it.'

Interviewers brought up her reputation for partying too hard. She explained that she'd reasoned at the time: if those around her were painting the town red, why couldn't she? Though she was under age, she was a success, with just as much right to celebrate that as the next person. And when people came down on her like a ton of bricks, moralizing and worrying, it only encouraged her to party twice as hard. But she was never out of control. The problem was that she'd grown up in the public eye. The transition from cute, innocent Billie to sexy, sassy, party-queen Billie was hard enough for Billie herself to experience, let alone everybody else.

She hadn't realized how shallow the music business was until she walked away. 'It's only when I come out of London that I realize how jaded we all are and how hard we've become and how fast we drink and how much we talk.'

She'd rediscovered her hatred of showbiz parties, denouncing them for the industry networking they facilitate and calling them 'dull'. They reinforced her view that taking time out was the only way to pursue a career in show business, as it allowed for a period of reflection, as well as providing a much-needed breather from the non-stop self-promotion.

Her routine at home was utterly domestic. She was a morning person, rising early, at about quarter to seven, and going to bed at a reasonable hour too. During the day, she would read, work out on the treadmill in the house and keep up with the household chores.

They both enjoyed reading, with Billie listing biographies, Jackie Collins novels and, unpredictably, philosophy among her tastes. But she confessed to finding the latter 'a bit testing': 'So I just let Chris read it and break it down for me.'

Talking to the *Swindon Advertiser*, the local paper which had followed her career, she enthused about coming back to see her friends at bars such as Longs and The Apartment. 'I have a great time – it is different from London where everyone goes out every night and it all kind of blurs into one. There is a real buzz on a Friday night in Swindon. I love the people. I have so many fun memories of the place.'

When she saw her old friends, she wanted to hear all about them. Sick of the London scene, where everybody's favourite topic was themselves, Billie was eager to hear her mates' stories and catch up on the gossip. That was just as absorbing to her as any of her crazy showbiz tales.

It was what excited her about village life with Chris, too. She raved to reporters about the discussions that went on in the local pub, finding the change from shop talk refreshing. Instead of being centred on battling egos and recitations of CVs, the gossip was about *real* life. One friend worked in pest control; another was a bee-keeper. Their anecdotes kept Billie entertained like no launch party ever could. Billie revealed a penchant for cookery too, whipping up desserts for the local fêtes. She relished the normality: 'It keeps my feet on the ground. Our jobs are so extraordinary and so silly, you need that leveller.'

She was happy to stroll to the pub in gardening trousers and one of Chris's jackets. This relaxed attitude to her appearance showed a happiness and satisfaction with life that the polished pop star Billie never achieved. Chris taught her to be laid-back about her looks and this outlook was one of the things she loved about him. Whereas in previous relationships she had fretted over her clothes, now she didn't worry. She knew it didn't matter – to either of them. It was a freedom that she savoured. Preened and primped by make-up artists and fashion girls for so long, Billie had never had the chance to develop a personal style. Now she rebelled against those teen years and made fashion choices that, while rubbished by the media for being the 'wrong' ones, were at least choices. She threw out the diet plans and ate whatever she wanted. She chose big sizes rather than opting for clinging catsuits. Where once she slimmed, now she put on weight. She jettisoned the red-carpet frocks and slinky outfits and stuck to tracksuits, T-shirts and raiding Chris's wardrobe instead. More than anything, she made a decision about the future: 'I don't want my career to dictate how I should appear or behave.'

She was open about her new attitude, proudly telling people that she washed her hair only once a week and that she liked the dishevelled look it gave her, revealing to *New Woman*: 'Chris says it's like waking up with Rod

Stewart because my hair is so bushy and big in the morning.' The truth was, Billie just couldn't be bothered any more. She'd had enough of high maintenance, now she just wanted to relax.

She wasn't ducking any questions, even about her drinking. 'I can't do one glass,' she admitted to *The Guardian*. 'I can only do two. One glass doesn't make any sense to me at all.'

With her career revitalized, though, she was barely drinking at all. She never drank on the job – partly because her short attention span wouldn't allow it. But she confessed that when she and Chris had first met it was party city, with plenty of boozy sessions. 'He had this whole life that he wanted to share with me and so many mates that he wanted me to meet, and a lot of that involved going out and meeting these really eccentric people and just having a great time.'

She was never concerned that they were drinking too much. As she pointed out, 'My friends go to university and drink solidly for three years.' Admittedly, Chris, a media mogul in his mid-thirties, was not the archetypal student profile, but twenty-something Billie felt she was just doing what everyone else her age was doing. As ever, she just happened to be doing it under the glare of the media spotlight.

She revealed that their party days were mostly behind them now. Living together and being happily married had changed their hectic social lives; they could stay in together and have a good time. And Billie was luxuriating in having a settled home life. But she still liked the odd drink: 'I love going out with the girls sometimes for a great bottle of cheap wine and just talking about … Well, it usually ends up with sex talk, doesn't it?'

She was even willing to talk about the ultimate celeb taboo – cellulite. 'Everyone's got cellulite. When you see these girls on TV, they look great – but do you know how hard they have to work at that? It's a complete lifestyle,' she said to *New Woman*. 'You can't look like that without really putting yourself through something weird and girls should realize that. It's like I say to my sisters: "Just because you put some weight on doesn't mean you're not a success." The more you starve your-self, the more your personality suffers, I think.'

Most of all, though, she wanted to talk about work. She talked about her training, how as a young girl audi-tioning for Sylvia Young's theatre school it was the acting that had been her main strength, her main ambi-tion. The singing was just her lucky break, the open door that would hopefully lead to other opportunities. Despite the training and the long-held ambition, it was still a daunting move: 'You don't realize the responsi-bility until you're on set, surrounded by crew and everyone's waiting for you to say a line.'

Success had not been automatic. 'I auditioned. I audition all the time. When anything's offered to me on a plate, when work's concerned, I get a bit like, "Why?" I never think I deserve anything really.'

The Miller's Tale featured a nude love scene with James Nesbitt. Billie had been unfazed. She followed her instincts on it and simply tried to do her best. Luckily, the scene was filmed towards the end of the shoot: by that time she felt relaxed with James and the crew working behind the scenes. Also fortunately, her husband wasn't bothered by it either. 'That's what's good about being married to somebody in this industry because those situations, I imagine, can be quite sticky otherwise … That's the advantage of going out with a man and not a boy. I think boys in their twenties are a nightmare to go out with because they are so insecure.'

Her BBC debut won outstanding reviews. Bonnie Greer in *The Mail on Sunday* wrote: 'It is Mrs Chris Evans who is the revelation. As Alison, the young wife, Piper lights up the screen to such an extent that you actually miss her when she's not there. Funny and heartbreaking at the same time, Piper sends up her own career as a singer with expert comic timing. Chris Evans could do worse than plough his fortune into a film career for his wife. With the right guidance, Piper could be a serious cinematic contender.'

Nesbitt was delighted at his co-star's ability. 'Billie is an original, and has something that's a bit of a cliché – people call it "star quality", but it's a very rare aura and presence as a person.'

'The camera loves Billie,' said *Miller's Tale* screenwriter Peter Bowker to *The Independent on Sunday*. 'I've seen it before, but never witnessed it so dramatically.'

The Guardian's Emma Brockes put it more grudgingly: 'At the party for *The Miller's Tale*, the attention of everyone in the room was compulsively drawn to Piper, although there were other actors present. She has the reflective quality of the seasoned celeb; that is to say, light bounces off her, or at least off her hard outer shell.'

Not everyone was surprised at her talent. Hugh Goldsmith, who still hoped to see his protégée return to the studio, had always known she was a natural actress. 'When I first met Sylvia [Young], she said Billie's talents were, in reverse order, singing, dancing and acting first. Sylvia said she was a little sad that a singing opportunity had come along and Billie wasn't pursuing her acting career.'

A friend of Chris warned in the *Daily Mail*: 'The work she's doing is being well received and people in the business are taking her seriously. She feels she absolutely has to make it on her own and is pursuing her career very actively. She is desperate for it to work and is very determined. If her career starts to take off, I should think that would make life quite interesting. If she did get a big break, there might be some element of competition between them.'

The breaks, though, still weren't going Billie's way. She was shortlisted for a part in Richard Eyre's film *Stage Beauty*, but Claire Danes got the role. 'It was up to me to prove I was very serious about what I wanted to do. It was a bit tough at times, but it was probably me thinking that some of those people know, or think they know, a great deal about my life – what underwear you wear, what time you fall out of pubs.'

The decision to start auditioning had been made while they were in Hollywood. 'I thought, "Now is the time to get an agent, get my ten-by-eights [photographs] and try to get a job."' She was desperate for a role in the remake of *Alfie*, opposite Jude Law, but Sienna Miller got the part. Screen tests for a superhero movie, *Fantastic Four*, also came to nothing. The biggest disappointment was a try-out for a Dickens adaptation: 'This was a kick in the balls – Roman Polanski's *Oliver Twist*, the part of Nancy. I was so gutted when I didn't get that.'

But she was under no illusions about what was going wrong. 'I did some really shit auditions. The scripts were great, I was shit.'

After *The Miller's Tale*, Billie shot another low-budget movie, playing an art student opposite Dougray Scott. It was called *Things To Do Before You're 30*, though it was made under the working title *You Don't Have To Say You Love Me*. Either way, it made little impact on release a year later and was not much better received on its re-release at the beginning of June 2006: 'Insightful as a shaving-cream commercial,' said *The Guardian*.

More promising was a second BBC drama, a one-off about teenagers growing up in care. Brian Hill, the director of BBC2's *Bella and the Boys*, said to *The Independent on Sunday*: 'I needed someone who could play a fifteen-year-old and a twenty-eight-year-old. I saw twenty-five, thirty actors for the role. She wasn't as experienced as some of the other people, but she had enthusiasm and an understanding – certainly of the fifteen-year-old. In the end, I thought she had something special. There's a steeliness there.'

Billie knew her leading role as Bella, a rebellious, foul-mouthed troublemaker, would force people to look at her in a new light and she poured her heart into the piece. She was eager to do more plays like that, commenting that gritty parts taught her compassion and patience. Before it could be screened, though, there was time for another holiday, in the Seychelles.

Chris's latest gadget was a hand-held video camera, and fellow guests watched in bemusement as they chased each other in and out of the sea, filming all the time. 'They are all over each other on the beach,' complained one, through pursed lips. 'They don't even stop touching during dinner.'

When they came home, they shocked the village by selling Hascombe Court to Boris Berezovsky, a Russian billionaire friend of Chelsea owner Roman Abramovich. Berezovsky paid £10 million, which meant a £4-million profit for Chris and Billie, who even got to keep Christmas Cottage, their love nest in the grounds.

Bella and the Boys sparked another burst of applause for Billie. She'd taken the part seriously and done her research, she revealed: 'We spoke to kids and people who had been in care and are now care workers themselves. It was pretty spot on … hard-core, heavy and insightful. It was three solid weeks working with kids from care homes and you're kind of blind or deaf to some of the things that people go through in life. You read about them in the papers, but you never really get inside the person's head, and so working with these kids that had such crappy starts to life made me think a lot and it was a great project to work on. I feel it was quite a true account.'

Professionally, this sort of material was exactly the kind she wanted to work with in the future, she told Rebecca Tyrrel on the *Express*. She wasn't interested in period drama, but wanted to focus on 'contemporary issues and young writers. I love seeing their take on the world. The young writers' show at the Royal Court is so inspiring, so fantastic. That is the kind of thing I love. They are touching on issues that have affected them. I feel very passionate about that.'

At this critical point in her career, Billie's determination to be taken seriously left an almost physical impression on anyone who met her. She was intensely focused. Interviewers who expected to meet the carefree, laid-back Billie of earlier days, the girl who was content to follow her husband wherever in the world his next whim took him, were bewildered by her resolution. Where had this avid sense of purpose been hiding? Had she really been mature enough to put this burning ambition on ice – and then retrieve it, as hot as ever?

'Anybody that knows me, knows that [acting] is what I started out doing,' she said to the *Express*. 'I left Swindon when I was twelve to go to theatre school so that I could act 24/7, and singing came along and I thought, "This is great – in the future I hope it will open doors for me," and sure enough it has. But I don't feel I have slipped into anything because acting is my chosen profession. It has always been in the forefront of my mind.'

The acting world was much more enjoyable than pop: the people were nicer and she felt she was closer to the heart of a creative process. Offers were slow to come and that upset her at first, but she understood that directors had her pigeon-holed as a singer and she would have to work hard to change people's preconceptions. She was constantly working on her technique: 'Reading about actors, watching their work, going to the theatre. For me, that is study. Not academic stuff, which frankly to me was so tedious. I have a short attention span!'

One thing was clear: the months of self-imposed silence had not dampened her gift for a memorable quote. Every time she opened her mouth to talk about acting, another quip went zinging. 'I'd love, love, love to win a BAFTA or an Oscar. They look fantastic – you just want to touch them.' And another: 'I'd like to play somebody quite schizophrenic. I like that idea of entering a completely different mindset.' And another: 'I don't feel like an alien when I'm acting.'

That last one had a touch of prescience ...

13 JUST WHAT THE DOCTOR ORDERED

In March 2004, the first rumours broke: Billie had been picked to play Doctor Who's assistant in a revival of the iconic TV series. One of the best-loved programmes ever made by the BBC, *Doctor Who* had fizzled out in the eighties, but a whole generation had grown up with Saturday teatime memories of the Doctor's struggle to save the world from Daleks, Cybermen and other alien invaders.

The Doctor always had a companion, a girl who joined him to travel through time and space in a blue phone box called the TARDIS. When writer Russell T. Davies was approached to relaunch the series, he knew that getting the right actor to play the companion was as essential as finding the right Doctor.

After months of speculation, the *Shallow Grave* star Christopher Eccleston had been confirmed in the title role. A respected actor who usually took heavyweight parts, he was about to become a household name. But whoever was picked to be his sidekick would have an even higher profile. Previously unknown actors such as Louise Jameson and Lalla Ward, who were companions when Tom Baker played the Doctor, were still remembered for the role, twenty-five years on.

A BBC insider said: 'They want a contemporary girl to play Rose to fit with the modern feel of this adaptation.'

Anna Friel, Keeley Hawes and Loo Brealey were all rumoured to be auditioning to play Rose, a shop girl who would be rescued from marauding mannequins in the pilot episode. But when Billie turned up to meet the producers, she got the part almost instantly.

Julie Gardner, newly appointed head of drama for BBC Wales, said: 'From the moment she walked through the door, we loved her because there's something very real about her. She's got glamour, she's very beautiful and she has a spirit about her which really comes through.'

The audition might have been a walkover, but Billie found it gruelling. After reading the part through for the first time, 'I had a recall and in my recall I had to read opposite Chris [Eccleston], which was absolutely terrifying. I mean, here's someone who I admired and it was just such a daunting experience. But he was so lovely, and so calm and collected, and we just got on famously.'

The news would not be confirmed for another six weeks; in the meantime *The Calcium Kid* was on release and Billie was trying out for a horror movie called *Spirit Trap*. And she was eager to talk about it all.

'I don't have to do things for the sake of them,' she insisted to Rachel Cooke of *The Observer*. 'I can wait a while, find the right things. I've got the time to go out and find out about life, observe people and dynamic situations that help me in my work. Ultimately, I'm only ever going to do the things that interest me, that I feel I can do something with. If that means people don't see it, that doesn't really bother me. I need to be part of things that make me feel alive. Even if I'm offered a blockbuster, it may not be right at the time, or benefit me.'

Her role as Angel opposite Orlando Bloom was 'a small part, but quite significant', she said. 'It was perfect for me, because it's my first film and I was nervous about the whole experience – I was terrified. I always am with things I care about. The adrenaline comes and I turn into this manic girl.'

Editors knew their readers were less interested in hearing shop talk, of course: what they wanted was gossip and revealing asides and glimpses of celebrity marriage. Billie was happy to meet any question head-on, even the downright rude ones – such as what she thought of her husband's many old flames.

'I don't really care. The ex thing never really bothers me at all. I'm me and he didn't marry them so that kind of says something. I've never asked him why he married me. You'd have to ask him,' she told *New Woman*'s Simon Cage.

Billie revealed that she tried to keep things fresh in the marriage, occasionally doing something that would surprise her husband. Not that she wanted to know what Chris liked about her, or what it was that had made him fall in love with her: she preferred to remain in the dark, fearing that she would become too self-conscious about whatever aspect he named.

Chris treated her with the same spontaneity, she added: 'He's really romantic, but not in a clichéd way. He'll bring me a surprise Starbucks coffee or leave me little notes – nice, unexpected things.'

One thing they didn't talk about, she said, was money. 'Money's never been a big part of my life. Chris and I never have conversations about money … We don't do all the designer clothes and the cars. Chris has got a collection of cars but it's just his hobby. We just spend it on holidays and have a great life. We can eat out when we want to and we don't have to think about the small things like getting in a cab and worrying about the meter. We're both from families that have nothing. We could survive again with nothing but it probably wouldn't be as much fun.'

That background had made her careful about spending, too. The instinct for a bargain was ingrained and she made her purchases last. The first treat she bought herself after hitting number one was a Gucci wallet and the extravagance of it had shocked her, but the wallet was still in her bag and she used it every day. Perhaps it lasted well because it wasn't opened too often.

She told *The Observer*: 'I have so much more fun with people than with assets. That's not to say I'm ungrateful. But the old cliché about it not bringing you happiness is true. And I don't have a love for fame. We don't travel with an entourage. I can't see how that would make life enjoyable. I had that as a pop star, and

I hated it. I'd rather be in the middle of things than in the VIP room.'

She knew people still tutted over the age gap between her and Chris and she cared as little as ever. When she and Chris married, 'I did register that not everyone else might get off on it, but I didn't care at all. When you do things for yourself, it's so exciting, it's so exhilarating. No one can tell you who to marry. And at the time, I was in love. I wanted to be with that person for ever. I found someone who loved me and I need that.'

That didn't mean she couldn't cope without him. Whatever the papers implied about her husband's over-bearing character and his dominance in the marriage, she knew that nobody owned her. She reassured Emma Brockes: 'I'd been on my own for so long before I met Chris. I'm still independent. I can sort myself out … if need be.'

Yet they were soulmates, she said, and that was partly because both of them were comfortable just as they were. 'Chris doesn't give a shit. There's nothing sexier than people who are confident or happy in their own skin. I hate men who are worried about appearance. It's so ugly. I hate shaving my legs and plucking my eyebrows. I don't care about all that shit. I have gym wear, sleep wear and going-down-the-shops wear, and sometimes I can be in that for days at a time. I think it has to do with having been primped and preened and groomed from the moment I left school … Kylie can keep the title Arse Queen and she can take hers down to the gym every day to get it buffed. I've got other things to do.'

So it wasn't vanity but professional demands that had put her on the Atkins diet, a stringent regime that forbade all carbohydrates. Critics called the diet unsafe, and claimed it could cause bad breath and constipation, but in 2004 it was the most popular food plan for celebs. According to Dr Richard Atkins, carbs in bread, pasta and potatoes produce glucose and glucose creates fat. Fatty foods like cheese, on the other hand, don't add weight and meat is ideal for slimming.

Billie, who had never warmed to Chris's vegetarian regime, discovered that the Atkins worked well for her. Not that it was easy. 'Maybe I'm not designed to be stick thin … I was brought up on bread and butter. Every meal, I would have two rounds. So suddenly, not having it as part of my diet is a bit like losing a friend. I find myself hanging round bakeries, inhaling the smell of the pastries. It's quite sad. The trouble is, getting rid of it really does make a difference. I feel much less guilty after I've eaten. Bread makes me feel like such a heifer!'

While Billie was juggling her filming schedule – in April, she landed the lead role of Jenny in the movie *Spirit Trap* – and her interviews, all without the benefit of a sandwich or a beer (or even her favourite meal, beans on toast – carbs are everywhere!), her husband's career was in the doldrums. Channel 4 dropped his £1-million show *Boys and Girls* in February, *Live with Christian O'Connell* had ended in acrimony and *The Terry and Gaby Show* – conceived as a rival to *Today with Des and Mel* and *Richard & Judy* – had delivered less than a quarter of a million viewers. Terry Wogan looked bored, complained reviewers, and Chris's old partner from *The Big Breakfast*, Gaby Roslin, was too shouty.

'Everything Chris touches is turning to mud,' said one friend to the *Sunday Mirror*. And there was a joke going round the media world that Chris had been overheard at the Groucho Club, London's meeting place for television types, telling a friend that he'd been working for the past fifteen minutes. When the friend asked if that was Chris's quota for the day, he replied: 'Yeah, and tomorrow.'

It wasn't a very funny joke, but Chris had made a lot of enemies who needed only the slightest excuse to gloat and sneer. When Jonathan Ross had mocked his former production assistant at the British Comedy Awards in December 2003, he got the biggest laugh of the night.

It wasn't surprising, therefore, as Billie settled into a new routine, first shooting *Spirit Trap* and then filming *Doctor Who* in South Wales, that whispers were starting about their marriage.

'Billie has made friends with lots of actor types, and Chris doesn't like going out with them,' one unnamed source on the *Spirit Trap* set told reporters. 'It means they are spending more time apart … She arrives on set at first light and leaves looking exhausted late in the evening. It's obvious to everyone Billie is hating being apart from Chris, yet he has the time and money to be there for her.'

In private, Billie did express frustration to friends that Chris wasn't around to support her, but she spoke barely a word of criticism in public. When she did, there were only the merest hints that her husband had become too stay-at-home. Billie would mention his fondness for reading, whereas she didn't have the patience at present to settle with a book. Or she'd bring up their different tastes in radio stations – he liked Radio 4, but she always tuned in to Kiss FM when she was driving. As always with Billie, though, she ended on an upbeat note, enthusing about how Chris's favourite station made her 'all cultured' and was 'really interesting'.

The news that Billie was to star in *Doctor Who* was officially announced in late May 2004, to front-page headlines – most of them punning that she was 'just what the Doctor ordered'.

Julie Gardner declared: 'We needed to find a unique, dynamic partner for Christopher Eccleston, and Billie fits the bill perfectly. She will make an extraordinary Rose Tyler. Doctor Who has his new assistant!'

Billie's response was formal, as if she was worried that her usual scattershot interview style would cause ripples at the BBC. '*Doctor Who* is an iconic show and I am absolutely thrilled to be playing the part of Rose Tyler,' she said. 'I am also looking forward to working with Christopher Eccleston and writer Russell T. Davies.'

Davies was the driving force behind the revival. His Channel 4 drama *Queer as Folk* had made him one of television's most in-demand scriptwriters, but he was steadfastly refusing to work for the BBC unless they let him bring back *Doctor Who*. A fan since childhood, he was certain that the characters and the concept were winners. The show had been discarded when its cardboard special effects were made to look comical by the computer graphics of Hollywood's *Star Wars* and *The Terminator* – but Davies knew that viewers wanted more than explosions in far-away galaxies.

Gardner agreed, enthusiastically as ever: 'It can go anywhere in time and space, and the main characters are an alien and a human, with all the confusion that brings,' she said. 'There's no story that can't be told.'

When she got the green light for the show, she called Davies to congratulate him – only to realize he was getting cold feet. 'He didn't say yes immediately,' she admitted.

'I actually spent three days thinking very seriously about it,' he said in a web-site interview. 'I love *Doctor Who* and part of me thought, "If you love something maybe you should leave it alone." But it was three days of nonsense really and my friends were slapping me round the head, and saying, "Don't be stupid, of course you've got to do it."'

He knew exactly how he wanted to play the scenes. 'The key word is fun. It's funny, scary, fast-moving, adventurous, but above all the new *Doctor Who* is fun. I watch a lot of other science-fiction shows and they tend to be very pious, sombre, dark, even angst-ridden, and that would just die a death on a Saturday evening. People want to be entertained at that time.'

Creating a pacy, witty show would be impossible without the right stars. A two-dimensional heroine could ruin the show. Davies, who was offered the chance to oversee the whole series as executive producer, with a hand in every decision, saw instantly that Billie was the right choice. 'The companion is as pivotal to these adventures as the Doctor himself – Rose can be our eyes, discovering spaceships and alien creatures with awe and wonder, and a vital sense of humour. Billie is absolutely perfect, and very close to the description of Rose on the page.'

Everyone was clearly overcome with excitement at both the regeneration of *Doctor Who* and the casting of Billie. But if the young actress was intimidated by the immense hype building up around her debut outing as the Doctor's assistant, she tried not to let it show. Though the programme had 'Billie's Big Break' stamped all over it, she didn't let the scale of the opportunity panic her. 'I deliberately didn't watch the DVDs of old episodes. So I didn't really feel the pressure of the fact that it's such an iconic show.'

She loved the thought of playing Rose and found a lot in the character that could come from her own experiences, as she explained to the *Radio Times*: 'Rose wants to try new things and wants answers. She's always asking "How?" and "Why?" and I relate to her in that sense. She's on a par with the Doctor. They teach each other. She's closed off from the world, but she could, potentially, be someone brilliant. He shows her how to do that. And equally, she shows him how to be sympathetic, how to have morals and express his emotions. It's an interesting dynamic … They're like a good friendship or a good marriage. Of course, you desperately want them to get together.'

Throughout the summer Billie focused all her energy on her acting. She was in Cardiff, where the shoot was based, all week long, week after week. This was her dream and she seized it with both hands. But it was a dream that came at a price.

14 BREAKING UP IS HARD TO DO

The story ran as an exclusive in every tabloid on Saturday 25 September 2004: Chris and Billie's marriage on the rocks.

The date was significant. The couple had been effectively living apart for two months, but though friends knew how little the pair were seeing of each other, no one realized how deep the estrangement had become until Billie's birthday on 22 September. She was twenty-two years old and she went for a meal with a female friend at the St David's Hotel in Cardiff.

'She looked really fed up and sad,' said one guest to the *Star*. 'There was no spark in her at all. You would never have known it was her birthday because she wasn't celebrating. She was tucked into a quiet corner, talking and smoking non-stop.'

Chris was in Los Angeles, meeting television executives. This would be the first time in four years that he had missed the date and though Billie didn't want to make a big deal of it – she had to do a night-time shoot between 2 a.m. and 6 a.m. the next morning – the fact he was on a different continent seemed symbolic of how far apart they had drifted.

Suddenly, reporters realized that this was more than a domestic row. This was a celebrity break-up, in a marriage that media-watchers had been waiting to bury for years. When the story broke, there was a feeding frenzy, but the clues had been piling up since the beginning of July.

The pace of filming had hit Billie hard. She had only done one-off shows as an actor and now she was making a thirteen-part series to a tight deadline – twelve-hour days, working eleven days out of every two weeks. It was a different world, but she immersed herself in it with her usual intensity. That didn't leave much time for trips back to London and when she did have a couple of days free she wanted to rest. One Friday evening, she was due to end filming late, but with the promise of a weekend off she invited Chris to join her in Cardiff. He refused: if she wanted to see him, she could drive the 150 miles home, he said. He couldn't be bothered with it.

When she did visit the two-storey apartment Chris had bought in Primrose Hill, north London, he sometimes sat for hours without speaking, or just grunting responses. 'He becomes uncommunicative when he's in one of his black moods,' said a friend. Billie didn't know how to lift him when he was down – if he wouldn't respond to her energy and cheerfulness, she couldn't reach him.

To break the cycle, Billie proposed a weekend break

abroad. They didn't have time to fly to the villa in the Algarve, so they stayed in a pension on the Normandy coast. One holidaymaker recognized them and cheekily shot some pictures of them on the beach. 'There was no doubt they were still in love,' Trevor Pidgeon commented to the *Mirror*. 'I even got the impression they were looking in the estate agents for a place to buy in France. At dinner Billie was sitting on Chris's lap and they couldn't keep their hands off each other. But when I saw them the next morning, Billie looked in a bad way. Her eyes were really puffy and she looked like she'd been crying or hadn't had much sleep. I thought they might have had a boozy row.'

Determined that she wouldn't slip back into the bad old ways of living in a hotel, Billie rented a Cardiff penthouse, close to singer Charlotte Church's pad. Neighbours, well used to keeping an eye open for celebrity visitors, noticed that Chris wasn't calling. 'I've heard Billie and Chris might split up and it doesn't surprise me,' said one. 'They have hardly seen each other at all. Chris has only been down to visit her about twice since she moved in. I've just seen fleeting glimpses of him. Every time I've seen Billie she's been on her own.'

Before he left for California, Chris did make a Sunday visit to the penthouse. Billie wound herself up to make the day buzz, ready to show him the restaurants she had discovered, to introduce him to her new friends, to show him over the sets. Chris walked in and switched on the television. He spent the afternoon watching the Ryder Cup.

'I've always supported everything Chris has done and now I'm working hard I wanted him to be there for me,' Billie was quoted as saying in the *Sunday Mirror*. 'It's just like he can't be bothered – he puts no energy into us. I'm tired and low, and I'm pissed off with him.'

The press, which hadn't understood the relationship from the start, decided there must be a more urgent cause for the break-up. By the Sunday, reporters were talking to anyone on the *Doctor Who* crew who would even say 'hello', but they couldn't uncover any scandals. When Billie told friends there was no one else involved, she meant exactly what she said.

Television crews are always full of gossip and stories began to circulate that Billie had been in tears during a heated mobile-phone conversation. Imaginative news editors wondered if Billie and Chris Eccleston had forged a bond that was more than professional – or if Chris Evans, volatile and insecure, suspected his wife of having an affair with her co-star. But the truth, as BBC insiders were happy to point out, was that there were personality clashes between several of the crew and Eccleston; while Billie got on better with him than some of the team, she was certainly not having an affair with the new Doctor.

Unable to face the press in Cardiff, Billie retreated to Swindon. Her grandparents still lived there and she spent Saturday night with her mum's father, David Hughes. 'I'm sorry, I've got no comment,' she told newsmen as she marched into the house.

David faced them a couple of hours later, on his way

She's back: Billie wows the critics as an actress. With Orlando Bloom in *The Calcium Kid* (*above*), and with Dennis Waterman (*left*) and James Nesbitt (*below*) in the BBC's adaptation of 'The Miller's Tale'. Billie wasn't fazed by anything.

Kiss from a Rose: Billie lands a leading role in *Doctor Who* in 2004, alongside Christopher Eccleston.

The part proved the kiss of death for her marriage with Chris Evans – but the couple remain close, pictured here in April 2006.

'When they said it was me, I was just amazed': Billie wins Most Popular Actress at the National Television Awards in October 2005.

With her *Times* Breakthrough Award at the South Bank Awards in January 2006.

Opposite page: Billie with new love Amadu Sowe.

Glamming it up in an *Arena* magazine photo shoot ...

Opposite page: Filming *Doctor Who*'s second series with her new co-star, David Tennant.

... and keeping it real at the V Festival.

With Russell T. Davies (*centre*) and David Tennant at the 2006 BAFTA Awards, celebrating their win for Best Drama Series and the Pioneer Audience Award.

At the VIP screening of her movie *Things To Do Before You're 30* in May 2006, with fellow actors Jimi Mistry (*left*) and Dougray Scott. Does Hollywood beckon for Ms Piper?

to the off-licence to get cigarettes for Billie. Asked how his granddaughter was, he replied: 'She's fine.' But when they asked if she and Chris had split up, he stonewalled: 'I wouldn't know anything about that.'

Deprived of fresh information, journalists started to speculate about a divorce settlement. After a series of disastrous TV ventures, Chris's fortune had dwindled, but he was still worth an estimated £30 million – and he had not asked Billie to sign a pre-nuptial agreement when they wed. She could expect an eight-figure divorce settlement. 'She doesn't want his money,' friends replied. 'She would never try to take him to the cleaners.'

The truth was that all their friends had come to see the marriage as something timeless, a never-ending romance between the most unlikely people in the strangest of circumstances. The love that bound Billie and Chris was guileless and innocent and to see it shatter would just be too sad. So instead of feeding the gossip machine, everyone who was fond of them closed ranks.

Most repeated a variation on this line: 'Up until now they've had a very solid relationship. They are a lovely couple, but things have been difficult recently. There have been rows and the pair are simply drifting apart. There's no one else involved. It is very sad, but their friends are all rallying round to help – no one wants to see them split up. Chris and Billie are trying to sort things out and they are just hoping that this is a blip. It would not be right to say that they have separated. Billie has been away filming a lot. Neither of them have moved out.'

TV insiders were less generous and claimed Chris was jealous of the way Billie poured her energy into her work. 'What has shocked Billie is the way Chris interpreted her working relationship,' said one to *The Mail on Sunday*. 'He has displayed such open jealousy that it has made Billie question the worth of her entire relationship with him. The last three months have brought out a side of Chris that Billie really hadn't seen before. She is worried that the jealousy is made all the more acute because his career is not exactly flourishing.'

The simmering resentment boiled over that September day when Chris arrived from London and switched on the telly to watch golf. On another occasion, it might not have been a big deal. What made this different was the offer Billie had recently had of a second *Doctor Who* series. She was going to spend another twelve months in Cardiff, playing Rose. And if eight weeks apart had done such damage to her marriage, what would a year do? Wasn't it kinder to put their relationship out of its misery straight away?

Chris didn't argue. He loathed confrontations. If the least painful path led to separation, then they would separate. But by saving himself the unpleasantness of a screaming row, he paid for it. 'Chris is in a terrible state,' one friend said, days later. 'His greatest fear has always been losing Billie. Despite all the bravado, he is actually very insecure.'

The day after the news broke on 25 September, Billie left Swindon and drove to north London, where she spent about seven hours drinking with friends at the St John's pub in Archway. Just to be away from the pressures of filming for a few hours was a tonic. 'She didn't seem to have a care in the world,' said one drinker. 'You would never have guessed that her marriage was in trouble.'

Chris, meanwhile, was at the White Horse in Hascombe, drinking lager, red wine and champagne, and singing songs with a party of about twenty pals. One of them told reporters: 'It's a difficult time for Chris and he just wants to have a few drinks with his mates to help him get through it. He doesn't see the point of putting pressure on Billie and reckons he might as well be in the pub. He says she won't have to look far if she wants to talk, but the ball's in her court.'

When Chris and Billie wed in 2001, his ex-wife Carol McGiffin's response was, 'I don't give a flying f**k whether he has got married. I don't know if they will be happy together. I don't even want to think about it.' Now a TV presenter on the *Loose Women* show, she commented on air: 'When I heard about the split I was rather upset. I was really sad. I thought he was going to be happy this time and it was all going to be lovely. But I said ages ago it would be all right as long as she was there for him when he wanted her to be. Now she's not there. She's working and he's not doing anything of note. Sadly, he's like that … He won't be liking it at all. He's at home in Surrey, she's in Cardiff, and I'm not remotely surprised by any of that.'

Did she think, asked another presenter, that Billie would be better off without Chris? 'Sadly, yeah … He's just not happy with himself. He did try therapy briefly when he was with me. He's not very good with himself. He simply can't be on his own. He's always running away. He's always having to be surrounded by people and he's wanting to get drunk all the time. He's got a load of issues he needs to sort out. I was so hopeful for him and Billie, but she's so young and he's starting to look a really old man.'

When shooting began again, in the middle of the week, the *Doctor Who* crew decided to cheer Billie up by throwing a post-birthday party. Fans who gathered to watch the filming said she looked relaxed between takes, but by the evening she couldn't face the party and cried off, claiming she had a headache.

Her mobile had been ringing all day and friends said Chris was making a concerted effort to talk her out of the break-up. 'She's going through a hard time,' said one crew member, 'but she has not let it interfere with her work.'

Billie repeatedly told Chris it was over. 'I really tried to make the marriage work, but there's just no hope,' the *Sunday Mirror* quoted her as saying. 'There's no way we can go back to the way it was. It's time to move on now. I just hope we can still be friends.'

She refused to let the stress stop her from enjoying herself and made a point of going to Ronnie Scott's jazz club in London ten days later to hear Madeleine Bell sing. 'Considering all she has been through recently, she was in very high spirits,' said another jazz fan. One of the men in her party kept leaning across to whisper in her ear. 'This guy obviously has the magic touch when it comes to cheering her up. Every time he whispered, she burst into a fit of giggles.'

But, just a short time later, on 22 October, the brave face faltered on a night out at London's Aura nightclub, when she was photographed looking the worse for wear, with glassy eyes and a tear-stained face. That day, she'd met Chris at the Groucho and had agreed to give the marriage another chance. She must have known it was a hopeless gesture, but after a heart-to-heart the next day at a favourite pub in Primrose Hill, they briefed friends to talk to the tabloids.

'We're reconciled, we spent the night together – it was great,' Billie told one. 'We're talking on the phone again and hoping to stay together.'

A friend of Chris's said: 'When they broke up last month, it was only for a cooling-off period. They always intended to try to make a go of it again. They never gave up hope of saving their marriage.'

But one month later, Chris confirmed the end of the relationship by deciding to set up a market stall in an attempt to sell off more than a million pounds' worth of their possessions.

It was an extraordinary way to announce a divorce. Everything connected with the life he had shared with Billie, the contents of their homes in Portugal, Surrey, London and Los Angeles, was for sale at Camden's Stables Market. His partner in the enterprise was Pete Winterbottom, an old friend; the sign over the warehouse door read 'Evans & Winterbottom, quality goods, established one day in the pub'.

The lots weren't cheap. A typical item was a leather bar stool, at £350. A black sofa once owned by Bob Dylan was offered at £4,250. Pete had the final say on prices, but Chris set the rules: 'Discounts will be given to people who tell us something we don't know and we don't sell to bad people. I think I know who the bad people are.'

Nothing from the marriage was sacred. A framed photograph of Chris and Billie dressed as cowboys, at Chessington World of Adventures before they were wed, was marked up for sale with everything else.

Emotionally, it was cathartic; financially, it was a disaster. Flying the furniture from LA cost £25,000, storage charges were £39,000, other transport costs totalled £24,000 and the stall itself cost £950 a week. After seven weeks Chris had raised just £21,000.

He was drinking heavily. On the first Sunday after setting up the stall, he suffered a severe nosebleed and spent five hours in the casualty department of the Royal Free Hospital in Hampstead. Despite warnings from doctors that alcohol consumption can raise blood pressure and cause bleeding, he then embarked on a six-hour drinking session, emerging from the Groucho Club at 2 a.m.

One friend said to the *Star*, 'We are really worried about Chris. He's always liked a drink, but a lot of people think he's been overdoing it since the break-up with Billie.'

Chris's mates had hoped that the hospital visit would slow the former DJ down a bit, that he'd lay off the booze for a while and chill out. But Chris clearly had different ideas. His friends thought the heavy drinking was having a negative effect, but he refused to listen to any advice. One friend said, 'He's a single man again and he won't have anyone telling him how to behave.'

Billie was coping better. She had a new boyfriend, a law student in his late twenties named Amadu Sowe. She had known him as a press officer at Virgin Records, but they didn't start dating until her marriage had broken down irretrievably.

A tall, attractive man with some style, Amadu was born in Camden, London, to a West African father and a Spanish mother. In contrast to Billie's former high-profile romances, this one was determinedly low-key. The pair were pictured on their way back from the supermarket, rather than on the red carpet. Amadu, his press officer training perhaps coming to the fore, was impressively discreet with the media, never giving a throwaway quote or an interview on the blossoming romance. Billie made it known that she was serious about him with an extravagant present – a £60,000 Porsche 911.

'Billie wanted to buy Amadu something really special as she knows he's gone to town on her, so she's ordered him the most amazing car,' said a friend to the *Star*.

The gift was clearly a symbolic gesture, with its echoes of Chris Evans's unconventional wooing of Billie. As her pal explained, 'Chris was then the one with all the power. Part of the reason their relationship stalled was because that balance shifted, so she's relishing her new-found role as a strong career woman. It's her way of saying, "I'm not a little girl any more – I call the shots.'"

15 LIFE AFTER CHRIS

Billie confirmed the marriage was over with a declaration of undying love for her ex. 'We've gone our separate ways as husband and wife,' she said to *The Sun* in December 2004, 'but we're still very much a part of each other's lives and always will be.

'Chris is the most amazing person I have ever met. I could never not have him in my life. He's so bright. He's constantly educating himself, seeing things and seeking things. Our biggest concern is for each other and that's it really. First and foremost, he is and will remain my best friend. Our relationship just ran its natural course. We just wanted to do different things in the end. It's really that simple. And it is sad. But we're just getting on with it.'

She spent New Year's Eve with Amadu, after introducing him to her parents. 'Mandy and Paul liked Chris an awful lot,' said a friend to the *Star*, 'but at the end of the day they completely understand that, if it wasn't meant to be, then that's life. They have been completely by Billie's side over the last few months, which have been pretty turbulent to say the least. They just want her to be happy. They're very proud of Billie.'

Billie knew that. 'My mum tells me she is when she's drunk! Then she says she is really happy for me and she loves me very much. My parents are not great with words, but they show me how they feel in other ways. They're there for me. There's none of that "I told you so", being disapproving, wagging fingers. They're just my mates and that's what I need.'

Mandy could have been a star too, Billie said. 'She's likeable, beautiful, talented – but softer than me, so I don't know if she could hack it.'

Billie made it clear that her priority was her acting career now. 'I fancy studying film-making in New York, a six-week crash course where I get to do some home-work and studying. I'm a bit of a boff at heart.'

Chris scrapped plans for a two-week stay at a health farm in the Yorkshire Dales and instead flew to LA. Friends said he was ready to try anything that might ease the stress he was feeling and was even considering acupuncture.

The first public comment on the break-up from Chris came in February 2005, after he was picked to present the BRITs. 'Billie's going to be on my table with my mum and Gazza [footballer and drinking companion Paul Gascoigne],' Chris told Louise Gannon of *The Mail on Sunday*. 'It's a really special night for me and she'd kill me if I didn't ask her to be there as part of it.'

The gesture underlined how close they remained. 'I love Billie. I really do. We're not married any more, but she's still the most fantastic woman I know, and one of a handful of people who are really important to me, and who I speak to all the time. Why wouldn't she remain a big part of my life? People seem surprised that you can stay friends after a marriage ends, but why not? People say all sorts of things about why we split up, but no one gets it right. It doesn't actually bother me. What is important to me is that we're OK and that's all.

'No one could have predicted how Billie's career was going to take off. None of us knew she'd turn out to be this amazing actress. She's brilliant. She's going to blow everyone away. But I knew that if we stayed married I'd hold her back and I didn't want to. Geography is very important in a marriage. It's never going to work if you are in separate places doing separate things. But more than that, I knew how important it was for her to go off and do her thing. If we were married I'd have wanted her to be with me and you just can't do that to someone. I want her to be happy and I want her to do well. If people can't understand that, then that's up to them. We're happy, and that's all I care about.'

The relationship remained volatile. One day they would be seen arguing in public, with Chris wagging his finger at Billie when she visited the market stall; the next, they'd be drinking and laughing together in one of their old haunts. When Billie called at the Primrose Hill apartment to collect some documents at 11 a.m. one morning in February, she had to bang on the door for more than ten minutes, yelling, 'It's Bill!' before Chris opened up. Amadu was parked around the corner, out of sight on a yellow line.

A woman later emerged from the house, speaking briefly to reporters to deny she was seeing Chris. One newspaperman said, 'It was like a scene from a farce. It took Chris a while to open the door, and he must have been mortified to realize it was Billie – especially as there was another woman inside.'

But days later they set out to the Washington pub near the apartment and spent an afternoon and evening drinking with friends.

'What's funny,' commented Chris to reporters, 'is that it's been said she's got a new boyfriend that I'm not supposed to know about. And I can't go out with her any more because every time I do, I try to snog her. But I'd rather have had three years with Billie than no years. She was too young for me – only eighteen when we met – but it was a real adventure. Our lives changed and although splitting up hurt, it was the best thing we ever did apart from marrying in the first place.

'I told her that if she gets married again, I'll be cheering loudest for her and she said she felt the same about me. I'd like to marry again. I'm envious when I go to the pub on Sundays and see families having lunch together. I'd like to have more kids. People who haven't got them seem miserable.'

Billie was in less of a hurry to start a family. She told Piers Morgan: 'I love the idea of going to New York and meeting someone there who I can fall in love with, then going to Paris maybe and meeting someone there ... I can see myself as one of those women who gets married about five times.' She wanted children, but not yet. 'I need to be a bit more settled and sure about the person I am with.'

Talking to the *Radio Times* a few months later, she expanded on her views: 'I'd love to have kids, but I don't know how people manage with a job like this. It's the one thing you really can't afford to f**k up. So many people have kids willy-nilly.'

As the *Doctor Who* launch neared, the publicity round began. Billie had never been a fan of the show as a child and decided that it was better to admit it honestly than to pretend – *Doctor Who* fans would spot a bluffer instantly. 'Obviously I understood the show and how iconic it was and its history,' she said to *Newsround*. 'I mean, we had it on in the house but I can't really remember sitting down with my family to watch it. But I just loved what was on the paper. I loved the script, and obviously the idea of working alongside Christopher Eccleston and putting Russell T. Davies's words into action was, for me, the greatest appeal.'

She would have been caught out by Christian O'Connell on his Xfm breakfast radio show if she had tried to pose as a Whovian, or *Doctor Who* geek. O'Connell, a fan of the show from childhood, asked whether Davros was in the new series, without explaining that Davros was the Daleks' creator. 'Who's that?' asked Billie. O'Connell was speechless, for about a quarter of a second. 'Oh, Billie!' he reprimanded her. 'Have a word with yourself.'

The launch was held at the St David's Hotel, with journalists entering through a mock-up of the TARDIS and Daleks patrolling the buffet. Earlier in the week, Billie had quietly issued a statement that she and Chris would divorce. Neither wanted to blame the other, so they would live separately for two years and part by mutual agreement. Billie did not intend to take any of her ex-husband's money, even though she would be entitled to millions. 'I'm not taking a penny of Chris's money,' she later said to Piers Morgan. 'I don't want his money, I just want his friendship. You can't put a price on that.'

And with that, the topic was closed.

At the launch, Billie insisted she wasn't worried about seeing her reviews, because she wouldn't be reading them. She told *The Independent on Sunday*: 'The way I approach my life now is – just don't read anything. Don't worry about things. Even reviews and stuff – if you believe the good ones, you've got to believe the bad ones. It's just my survival kit. I'm not in it for fame or money. I'm just in it because I love it. That's a really reassuring thought.'

She even claimed she wasn't concerned about being seen as a 'proper actor'. 'It might be nice,' she shrugged. 'But I'm not really that bothered either way. Because as far as I'm concerned, I am a serious actress. I don't need any validation from other people to convince myself that that's what I am.'

Batting aside the heavier questions, she showed that her teenage training with pop-mag questionnaires had stayed with her. Challenged to say where and when she'd go in her own TARDIS time machine, she didn't miss a beat: 'I'd like to see what my thirties look like, not too far – we're talking about eight years down the line. I'd like to see what's going on in my life – that's quite interesting to me.'

She did time-travel when certain songs came on the radio, she confessed, reminders of growing up in Swindon. 'I still get nostalgic when I hear a song that reminds me of sitting in a car park eating a hamburger,' she told Craig McLean of *The Independent on Sunday*. 'But I just didn't want to do that, I didn't want to be there. I wanted to be in London, or in America. And I wanted to work. My dad always had such an amazing work ethic, it was something I wanted.'

It wasn't her work ethic that had sustained her through the final, exhausting weeks of filming, though. 'I'm just surviving on coffee at the moment. Thank the god of coffee. It's my biggest vice right now.'

McLean was one of the first journalists to acknowledge that Billie, who had been written off as another pop casualty after her wedding, was the only star of the Girl Power generation who had taken her career to a new level. Unlike the members of the Spice Girls and All Saints, who had settled for varying degrees of celebrity-for-celebrity's-sake, Billie was developing.

She had no intention of ever going back to music. 'It gives me the fear, just thinking about it. I'm so glad I took two years out of the industry to go and see what life was really about. If I hadn't done that, I would probably still be a pop star. For two years we travelled shitloads and saw some stuff together. Most of the time we were on the road. It was so liberating and just the time of my life.

'We did it for as long as we needed to do it. And then it was like, "Right, we need to think about trying to do some work now." And we wanted to work because we felt completely inspired by what we'd seen, what we'd learned and the people we'd met. It was the most amazing experience. [For the first time] since I'd left school, I was doing exactly what I wanted to do, and on my own terms. That was very exciting. I had been groomed and made-up and, you know, having to be awake and in tune every day – I quite enjoyed just being a free spirit and not really giving a f**k.'

Christopher Eccleston was keen to acknowledge that Billie was much more than the usual Doctor Who companion. 'The Doctor's always been a hero,' he told journalists in a rare statement, 'but there's no heroine out there for eight-to-twelve-year-old girls. Now they've got one. Billie carries the series with me. We do it together, a man and a woman.

'I think we were well cast – very cleverly put together. We had a great time even though it was hard. We didn't know each other and we were together for eight months, six days a week, fourteen to fifteen hours a day, both with our careers on the line. I think we did really, really well. Rose is a heroine. She saves the Doctor's life in the first episode. There are huge emotional episodes and I think Billie pulled it off. As far as I'm concerned the Doctor and Rose love each other. I think it's love at first sight but it's not perhaps a conventional love affair. It's far more serious than that, as is love, I suppose.'

Billie was just as eager to praise her co-star, calling him 'an amazing man to work with. Christopher is somebody I'd been in awe of for ages. But he's not intimidating or patronizing in any way – he's taught me a lot.

'Christopher and I have shared so much during the past eight months. We had heavy schedules and personal lives and we've been joined at the hip. We have a very intense kind of relationship. We get on famously. It was instant – it just worked straight away.'

According to BBC insiders, however, it was rather more complicated than that. Rumours that Eccleston was not completely happy in the role were rife from the first days of shooting, but even so his decision to quit the series came as a bombshell – especially to the marketing department, which suddenly had lorry-loads of Doctor Who action figures that were out of date even before they hit the shelves.

'Billie and Christopher Eccleston really weren't getting on by the end of the first series,' reveals Matthew Sweet, a writer and broadcaster who presented *Night Waves* on Radio 3 as well as reporting for BBC2's *The Culture Show*. He is also an ardent Whovian with an official *Doctor Who* audio play, *Year of the Pig*, to his name, and he watched with fascination, and exclusive access to the set, as the new series came together.

In fact, relations on the show were rather strained in the uniquely pressurized environment. Matthew Sweet suggests, 'Christopher had a lot of power on the set. A lot of people who had to work with him weren't that sorry to see him go after one series, and I understand

Billie was one of them. Of course she's been terribly diplomatic about it, but she was rather relieved. It's certainly not true, as several of the tabloids suggested, that Billie and Christopher were having an affair – there's nothing at all in that.'

Billie skirted the problem by discussing Rose's relationship with the Doctor instead. She explained that her character could show the hero how to explore unfamiliar emotions, while soaking up his knowledge and expertise. If that was a metaphor for how she dealt with the actor himself, she was far too well versed in speaking to reporters to let a slip of the tongue betray her.

'There has never been a relationship like this between the Doctor and his assistant before. It's a relationship you can't ever put your finger on. There's lots of holding hands. In the past the other Doctors have been slightly chauvinistic and patronizing to their assistants. But in this case they're on a par. He can be cold as ice at times and Rose finds that really hard to deal with, but he learns a lot about humanity through her.

'I took the part because I could relate to Rose. I was very similar – I realized I wanted something to happen in life, a bit more than I had. I wanted to find someone or something to challenge my ideas and broaden my horizons, so I definitely tapped into that. It's that feeling of wanting something to happen and not knowing how to go about it. I felt that when I was in Swindon at the age of fourteen – I wanted to get out. Rose is the same … It just takes a 900-year-old man in a blue box to get her going!'

The only tensions on the set that she was prepared to discuss were trivial ones. 'I've been really terrible at stunts,' she admitted to *The Sun*'s Sara Nathan. 'Every time I've done one I've messed it up and ended up trashing the set and props. I was so bruised and I've broken so many props, it's a joke. I just look at a prop and I start shaking – as does the prop. Towards the end I really messed my knee up.'

Despite her difficulties with props, she was still rather taken with them. 'It's so tempting to take stuff. I haven't got a Dalek as yet – but I'm working on it. There are wires that come off the walls in the TARDIS and I have an artist making me TARDIS-wire bracelets. My God, I could have a sonic screwdriver on my dressing table but I've been able to restrain myself.'

The relationship the tabloids really wanted to unravel, though, was with the other Christopher, her estranged husband. Had *Doctor Who* exterminated her marriage?

'I don't blame the job,' Billie insisted to the *Mirror*. 'I think whatever happened between Chris and I would have happened in the end anyway. I would never, ever say the job was responsible for my divorce – that would be stupid.'

She also shrugged off Chris's suggestion that she had been too young to get married and that the age gap had been too wide. 'I really don't know if that's the case. We had a great time while we were together and that's all that concerns me. We're best buddies and we always will be.'

The exhausting shooting schedule had helped her through the pain of the break-up. 'My focus was my work. The schedule has been so demanding, I had to stay focused. I threw myself into it 100 per cent. That was my plan. I don't know how I coped with it – I just seemed to. When something as heavy as that happens, you do throw yourself into your work. When you're working with a crew for eight months, you're in a bubble. I was pretty much oblivious to everything going on outside *Doctor Who*.' The show would have suffered if she had let her emotions override her responsibilities, she said. 'But the split has not been as tough as everybody thinks. It's all friendly, there are no bad feelings or resentment. It's very amicable. Chris has been nothing but supportive and I'm going to send him a tape of *Doctor Who* to watch.'

16 THE SWEETNESS OF SUCCESS

The applause for Billie was deafening. Viewers loved her, with more than 10 million people tuning in to watch each week, trouncing *Ant and Dec's Saturday Night Takeaway* on ITV, which could barely muster 7 million. Die-hard Whovians were forced to admit she might be the Doctor's best ever companion. And the team behind the show couldn't sing her praises loudly enough.

'She will go all the way to Hollywood after this,' predicted Russell T. Davies. 'She has got an amazing screen presence. She's got strength. She is like Brigitte Bardot. In fact, in one of the episodes they make her up to look like Bardot and it works. It's incredible to think that she is only twenty-two. She surprised me because I was expecting this jumped-up pop star. In fact she is very professional and extremely dedicated. I couldn't have asked for more from her. We were delighted with her performance. She has got so much to offer, I know she will go far. I think in five years' time, we'll be sitting discussing her Hollywood career.' He compared her to Catherine Zeta Jones, who had starred as Velma Kelly in the movie of the musical *Chicago*. 'Billie could do that, if she wanted to, and she will get parts like that. Acting that good always finds work.'

Despite her claims that she never read her own reviews, Billie couldn't ignore acclaim like that. She enjoyed it, thought about it, talked with a few close friends about it and then responded … by quitting the show.

Already reeling from Eccleston's departure, her BBC bosses were dumbfounded. They believed the show could cope with a new actor as the Doctor – after all, there had been eight others. But Billie was the surprise star and without her the second series might implode. Tabloid gossips immediately began bandying about new names – Rachel Stevens of S Club 7, *EastEnders'* Michelle Ryan, Rachael Stirling from *Tipping the Velvet* – but none of them had Billie's instant appeal.

Officially, the Beeb was in denial: 'Billie is definitely returning for the second series and will be in a number of episodes, but I can't tell you how many,' said a spokeswoman.

Unofficially, it was in panic. 'Billie is leaving,' whispered an insider. 'She will feature in some episodes of the second series, but her character won't be the companion by the end. It would appear she has already made up her mind. She is a great actress, but she does not want to become typecast.'

The announcement came as Billie was busy filming a modern adaptation of *Much Ado About Nothing* for the BBC. She played Hero, who in this version was a weathergirl.

Her agent, Michael Foster, admitted to a BBC executive that she was the most ambitious performer he'd known in more than twenty-five years in show business – but that didn't mean she was heading straight to Hollywood. Her friends hinted to gossip columnists that she wanted to spend some time in Africa, perhaps going to Ghana to work with the Make Poverty History campaign.

But a clear signal that she had no intention of moving to either America or Africa just yet came a few days later. Tired of living in a rented apartment, Billie went house-hunting. The old flat had had one handy advantage – it was within 200 yards of her former home with Chris, so she could beat London's parking problems by leaving her white Porsche on his drive.

The solution was obvious. She bought a house in Primrose Hill – a £2-million property almost directly opposite Chris's place. He even joined her for the viewing. What she always said to reporters was true: 'We're the best of buds and always will be. I always thought it was weird, when exes hung out together. Now I'm doing it myself, I understand it. It's almost nicer now because there are no harboured feelings, no resentment.' She emphasized she would not be taking a penny from Chris in their divorce settlement – to sue for his money would be 'disgusting'.

With her accommodation sorted out, Billie turned her attention back to business. Julie Gardner and the rest of *Doctor Who*'s executive team had already broken the bank to replace Chris Eccleston, by offering *Casanova* actor

David Tennant a £450,000 fee to become the tenth Doctor. Now they realized that the only way to keep Billie on the show was to pay her more – a lot more.

Doctor Who was proving a costly triumph. The corporation's head of drama commissioning, Jane Tranter, warned that the budget for other dramas would have to be slashed by 15 per cent … and that was before Billie's new salary had even been considered.

Matthew Sweet believes the BBC had no choice but to lure their star back. 'It's really her show. The BBC would do anything to keep her. Billie is very different from all of the other assistants. Whenever a new assistant has joined the cast in the past, the writers have promised, "This one is going to be more proactive, this one isn't a screamer, this one isn't going to fall over and twist her ankle," and often that has been true of the first few shows. They start out with good intentions and then they revert to stereotypes – at least, that's always what the actors who played them have said. Here, they have actually succeeded, because the show is built more around the companion character than around the Doctor. She is the line of continuity through the series.'

Fans were well aware of her unique appeal – as was the BBC, which finally agreed a new salary with the ambitious Ms Piper. Matthew Sweet recalls the first time he spoke to her, in a hotel in Cardiff, when he was making a film for *The Culture Show* about *Doctor Who*. He was there to talk to Russell T. Davies about the show's spin-offs and was waiting in the hotel bar when he belatedly realized that he was sitting next to the programme's star. Though he knew Billie was involved – he'd seen clips of the show, including a preview of the first episode – he hadn't at first noticed the young actress by his side. 'I'd looked at her and I think I'd even said hello to her and then turned round and talked to the person I was with. The key to her appeal is that there is not this strange aura around her. She actually looks like other people do. She's quite easy to miss sometimes. When you see her on the screen that works very well for her. There are a lot of girls that age who look like Billie Piper. It's the girl-next-door thing. This is the secret of her acting too – she has found some way of translating something very ordinary on to the screen.'

The new Doctor, David Tennant, was just as impressed. By the middle of July 2005, it was known for certain that Billie would be around for all of the second series and he was delighted. 'I didn't know her before,' he admitted, 'but I've been admiring her in the show. She's just great, fantastic. Just absolutely perfect. Spunky and quick and sexy, just the ideal companion really.'

A lifelong *Who* fan and an admirer of Eccleston's lugubrious style, Tennant often claimed he'd been inspired to start acting by his love for the show. Ever since he was four years old, he'd dreamed of playing the Doctor and now he was being offered sackfuls of money to live that dream. It seemed, he said, 'hilarious and impossible'.

Matthew Sweet sums it up. 'He's a complete *Doctor Who* nut. He's grateful for it, whereas Eccleston's involvement was more problematic: there was always a

sense in which he had no real affection for the programme. This was him letting his hair down and
showing he could do something less earnest than usual.
For Tennant, this is a dream job and he'll stick with it
for as long as they'll let him.'

As the shooting schedule gobbled up her summer,
Billie had little time for the sideline projects she'd been
pursuing, such as the launch of her horror movie, *Spirit
Trap*. She pleaded previous commitments as she cried
off the low-budget film's premiere, though her co-stars
grumbled that she was trying to put some distance
between herself and a stone-dead turkey. The 15-
certificate film had been slaughtered by critics for its
dull script and predictable plot. ('I was glued to my
seat,' said the *Mirror*'s critic. 'I mean that literally … I
really did have to glue myself to my chair to stop myself
walking out.')

She found time to spend a weekend at the V Festival,
Virgin's music extravaganza, with Amadu and James
Nesbitt. 'This is my first time camping,' she said to the
Mirror. 'My little brother's here with me and is really
excited!' She made a point of sharing the full festival
experience, even queuing for the public toilets. When a
security guard offered to escort her to the VIP loos, she
told him, 'I'm happy to wait like everyone else.'

Billie was buzzing. The weekly rave reviews for
Doctor Who were boosting her confidence, even though
she couldn't bring herself to sit down on a Saturday
night with the rest of the nation and tune in. 'I'll wait
for it to come out as a DVD box set,' she joked.

She controlled her career, her audience loved her and the future looked fantastic. The past was firmly behind her: 'I had an amazing time [in my teens], but it was also pretty horrible. That's why I was so happy to walk away, to go off and try to reinvent myself. I never really wanted to be a singer in the first place. I just wanted to act.

'I have to say I'm feeling pretty fearless at the moment,' she added to the *Mirror*. 'I feel I've nothing to lose. I've got six years' experience of this industry under my belt, so now I'm just going to go for it.'

She even claimed cheekily that she'd never intended to quit during the second series – she just couldn't quite believe that Russell T. Davies was going to script Rose into all thirteen episodes and she'd wanted to see the finished storylines before telling the world she was signing up for the duration.

'She definitely knows how to play the game,' Matthew Sweet comments wryly, 'but that's because she's been doing it for so long. She was sort of whelped into this culture and she's never lived out of the spotlight. She deals with attention in a way that's so confident and casual – I don't think she's a two-faced person, she really is like that. The ease with which she can deal with intrusive or aggressive journalists frightens me a little.'

Filming ended on the BBC Shakespeare adaptation just days before Billie returned to Cardiff. The David Nicholls script, relocating the Bard's characters to a regional TV newsroom, had delighted her, as she explained in a press release for the show: 'It's so funny, and every line in the script is a corker. I really enjoyed it. I thought it was a great concept. At drama school we studied Shakespeare three days a week; I think Shakespeare dominated about four years of my life and, at first, I used to find it so daunting. The thought of sitting down with a Shakespearean text used to scare me. But then I went to theatre school and it took on a whole new life. I became a huge fan. So when the script was floating around, I was quite keen to get a look at it. It's so good, and when I heard that Sarah [Parish, of *Cutting It*] and Damian [Lewis, from *The Forsyte Saga*] were involved, I knew I'd be in good company. It was an ensemble piece and we all gelled and got on so well – that was one of the highlights.'

In her favourite scene, at a fancy-dress ball, she was made up as Marilyn Monroe in the classic white dress from *The Seven Year Itch*. 'She's always been one of my heroes – I love Marilyn Monroe and I've had this small obsession with her, so I felt right at home in the wig and dress.' But Billie's disastrous relationship with props caused chaos once more when she had to don a pair of angel's wings. 'I nearly took out every member of the crew when I walked in at first with these bloody wings on my back!'

Two things worked well for her: the previous experience of working with Russell T. Davies's extraordinary scripts and her diligent approach to research. To get the intonation just right for her weathergirl role, Billie quizzed presenters. One weathergirl showed her footage of her early days in the studio. 'That was really beneficial. There are certain ways to hold and present yourself and there's also a rhythm in the way news reporters speak – you have to get hold of that. And then I just watched daytime TV solidly for about a week!'

But when she came to speaking some of the technical terms, such as 'altostratus castellanus', she needed to call on everything she'd learned in *Doctor Who*. 'Midtake, you'd find your top lip curled and you'd be sweating like a pig,' she confessed to the BBC press office. 'Those lines really did give you the fear. But I was getting used to saying words that I'd never used in my life, words that weren't in the dictionary – just made-up, Russell T. Davies words – so I started to get better and better at pronouncing the difficult ones.'

When the play was screened to rapturous reviews, no one who knew Billie was surprised. Peter Bowker, who had written the *Canterbury Tales* adaptation that launched her acting career, said only TV producers who hadn't been paying attention could still imagine she was 'some fluffy bunny who laughs in the right places and will be a bit vacuous. The other misconception is that she wouldn't have a sense of humour about where she is and where she's come from. In *The Miller's Tale* she was playing a singer, married to an older man. But, for all that, there was clearly proper acting going on. People came to me time and time again, saying she blew them away. Now whenever I'm in casting discussions, her name always comes up.'

The first show on the shooting schedule in Cardiff

was the *Doctor Who* Christmas special. Billie loved it, as she revealed to *The Observer*: 'I'm an absolute Christmas freak! I love the fact it starts in October now! However, this year for me it started in July as we were filming the Christmas special. It was slightly bizarre filming snow scenes in the middle of summer, but I was thrilled. It was great to start filming series two with this amazing, emotional and scary episode.

'I'm a huge fan of Christmas specials. It means so much to me that our show is going to go out on Christmas Day when all the families will be sitting down together, eating copious amounts of chocolate and drinking sherry. I have to be honest – I think I'm going to need a few sherries before I sit down to watch it, though!'

Little did she know it, but Christmas for Billie Piper was about to arrive early.

17 ON TOP OF THE WORLD

Billie had always wanted to win awards. She made no secret of it – an Oscar would be best, but everything was welcome. When she was named Most Popular Actress at the National Television Awards in October 2005, she could hardly believe it was happening.

'It was the most amazing feeling. I was so terrified, and I really thought one of the soap actresses would win. But when they said it was me, I was just amazed,' she said in her press interviews afterwards. 'I had to have a word with myself on the way to the stage because I thought I was going to cry and that would just be too embarrassing. It was a brilliant night but I spent the evening in shock, chewing my nails. It was such a strange, wonderful evening. I felt like I was having an out-of-body experience. Winning an award like this, which has been voted for by the public, makes you realize the enormous impact the series has had on the nation.'

Her first reaction as she carried her trophy back to her table was to call Chris Evans. 'I jumped in a cab to come and celebrate with her,' he said. Chris arrived in time to see *Doctor Who* win two more awards: Best Drama, and Most Popular Actor, for Christopher Eccleston.

'I'm thrilled for her and I knew she'd win,' her ex added. 'The great thing about our relationship now is we're best of friends. There aren't any arguments or problems – we can just enjoy each other's company. Some people think that's weird, but I like weird.'

But then the emotion of the occasion became too much for him.

'I'll always be bitter about *Doctor Who* because it ruined my marriage,' he said starkly to the *Star*'s reporters Charli Morgan and Mark Jefferies. 'When Billie got the job as Rose, she was always in Wales, so we were never together. And you don't get married to be apart – that's what I think anyway. But she knew we wouldn't see each other when she accepted the role, so I guess our fate was sealed then. It would be interesting to see if we'd still be together if she hadn't done the show. I don't know. I guess our marriage was coming to an end anyway. I can't watch the show without the tears coming.'

Billie, on the other hand, was sounding positive about staying with the show. 'I will definitely be in the whole second series. I hope I can stay on longer than that. I would really love to.'

But two weeks later, she did it again. Every tabloid's front page carried the story: Billie quits *Doctor Who*.

The BBC, claimed a source with a taste for understatement, 'are quite miffed about her decision'.

Miffed? Poleaxed was a better word.

Billie's agent hinted that the time was right for her to step on to a bigger stage. With a national award in the bag, she was more marketable than ever and Hollywood was beckoning.

BBC sources let it be known they were looking for a replacement. 'The casting people have been conducting secret auditions with a small number of actresses and keeping it very, very quiet. They are after a relative newcomer so this is the role which puts her in the public eye. It also means she's less likely to get bored after one series.'

Billie wasn't fooled. The BBC wasn't going to draft in any 'relative newcomer' to replace her. She held out for a better fee – and won a reputed £1.6 million to stay for the third series, eclipsing even David Tennant's £1.3-million pay packet.

And that wasn't the whole of the deal. Days later, she was named as the star of a prestigious drama based on bestselling novelist Philip Pullman's Victorian-era stories.

'She certainly has been very canny about the way she has made *Doctor Who* work for her within the BBC,' says Matthew Sweet. 'She got this new part as Sally Lockhart after the project was all up and running. She was parachuted into that because she saw it and heard that it was being done and thought, "I fancy that." There were people on the production team who felt so strongly that Billie Piper was not the right person for the part that at least one of them resigned, but she got the part anyway. It was imposed from above. She's been such a hit in *Doctor Who* that at the moment she can ask for anything she wants. It tells you something about the BBC's determination to promote her, but it also shows you what she can demand – as a price for staying in *Doctor Who*.'

Sally Lockhart is the heroine of *The Ruby in the Smoke*, the first of four Pullman tales. As filming started in May 2006, immediately after series two of *Doctor Who* finished shooting, it was clear that Billie was prepared to work tirelessly to cement her career. She was thrilled to be working with veteran actor Julie Walters on the project, though she admitted to the *Radio Times* that she was too embarrassed to tell the older woman how much she admired her.

Laura Mackie, head of BBC drama series and serials, was adamant that Billie had won the role on merit. 'Billie Piper is an extremely versatile actress whose talent has deservedly been recognized by critics and audiences alike ... Billie is the perfect choice for bringing to life this engaging and fearless heroine.' The deal was rumoured to be worth about £250,000 – with a second drama, *The Shadow in the North*, to follow.

David Tennant couldn't speak too highly of his co-star, gushing to *The Observer*: 'She's just perfect. She was so welcoming and easy to work with. I really think she is a brilliant actress, too: in every take she's got something new, she makes it look effortless.'

Billie's relationship with David Tennant was clearly blossoming, on both a professional and personal level.

But the rapport of the lead actors wasn't the only change on this second series. The crew were more confident and experienced and across the whole production there was a better atmosphere, making the programme much more fun to film. As Matthew Sweet explains, 'At the beginning it was very much a process of finding out how you make this programme again. There was only one person who survived from the old production team and it's the most complicated programme on TV. Even though the budgets are now much bigger, it's still done incredibly fast considering what you have to get up on the screen and nobody really knew quite how you made a show like that.

'It was difficult at the beginning, with lots of health-and-safety problems: they had people passing out inside costumes. There was a bit of a revolt from the actors who played the monsters because they felt they were being put in danger. This time round they know where they are, they know how long it takes to do a certain type of scene and they know how long you can leave somebody wrapped in plastic in a hole in the ground or whatever.'

At the beginning of 2006, the BBC announced it had sold screening rights for *Doctor Who* to the US Sci-Fi channel in a £3-million deal. That fuelled speculation that as Billie's profile rose in the States, she would find the lure of America too strong to resist. Although her fans would be as sorry as anyone at the BBC to see her finally carry out her threat to quit the show and head for Hollywood, some observers also feared that her big-screen career might not be the automatic success that some predict, and that she might be better served by staying in England. Matthew Sweet, for example, expresses some doubts: 'I'm always very sceptical about Hollywood. What happens to a lot of British actors is that they leave really good TV series and make a load of crappy films. It would be a shame if that happened to Billie. I don't really understand why being a TV star isn't good enough. The material can be a lot better and more substantial – you get a lot more lines.

'I'm also not sure that her persona is suited to international productions. You can imagine how difficult it would be for her to keep that laid-back lifestyle in Los Angeles. And part of her appeal is that there's something extravagantly ordinary about her. You can see that her skin's not that great, you can see her zits a lot of the time, and that's got a lot to do with the rigours of the schedule. She doesn't have that film-star skin, she wears too much make-up, you can see her roots, and I think this is all good. This is why people like her: she's not a remote figure. But I don't think Americans have an appetite for that. They wouldn't get her.'

Peter Bowker, writer of *The Miller's Tale*, shared those same worries with *The Independent on Sunday*. 'I don't know that Hollywood quite understands how attractive Billie is and her look. And she doesn't strike me as the sort of person who would go to LA to hang around to get the odd part, in the hope of getting a really good part in something like *Traffic* or *Chicago*. She strikes me as someone who needs to be working and needs to be doing interesting stuff.'

Billie herself insisted to the *Mirror*: 'I love what's going on here. There's some great telly at the moment and really smart writers. I'm happy where I am.'

Russell T. Davies hinted he might have the ultimate enticement to keep Billie with the show – by making her the eleventh Doctor. 'I'd have the nerve to make the Doctor a woman,' he said. 'I don't see why it couldn't be done.'

Another prize added glitter to Billie's grin in January when she won *The Times* Breakthrough Award at the South Bank Awards. The trophy honoured her achievement in staging a showbiz comeback in a new field after so long away from the limelight. 'I care so much more about acting than I do for music,' she said as she collected the award. 'I'm having the time of my life at the moment and this just makes it even better. *Doctor Who* has affected me personally. The stories are amazing, but it's bloody hard work … It's an exciting time for me to be alive and I am doing something that I have wanted to do since I was a kid. That means so much to me and I can't quite believe it is happening. I'm loving it. The fact that I am working as an actress every day makes me really happy.'

She was not just doing any work, either – shooting *Doctor Who* continued to present her with fresh challenges. In a scene where the two-dimensional villainess Lady Cassandra, who is nothing but a piece of stretched skin, possesses Rose's body, Billie's line was: 'Curves! Oh baby! It's like being inside a bouncy castle!'

And then she had to grab Tennant and kiss him.

'It was the first time I was trying to pull off comedy,' she said to *The Sun*. 'That really scared me as I've never done anything like that. Last year the Doctor got lots of the jokes so this year Russell gave me some good gags.' Though Billie had sent herself up in *The Miller's Tale*, this sort of comic acting was very different. Rather than making people laugh *at* her, she had to make them laugh with her. She was loving every moment of the filming process. 'It's a different series, I've been working with a different guy and my life has moved on, so it's cool. I'm glad the show was received so well last year and that's given us a pep in our step. To have such a huge success on our hands made this year more exciting and everyone was gagging to get back. So yeah, everything's sweet!'

The only cloud in her sky was a trivial niggle: she hadn't been nominated for a BAFTA. The British Academy of Film and Television Arts awards were the highest honour she could hope for in her current role as Rose and it was galling to be passed over.

'I'd have loved a BAFTA,' she said to the *Express*. 'I really wanted to be nominated. I was disappointed. The BAFTAs are special and it would be a lie if I said I wasn't bothered. But I suppose I have the rest of my life to get one, so I'm not going to get too hung up on it.'

She was still seeing Amadu – the pair were now living together – but spent a happy afternoon strolling round Primrose Hill with Chris to celebrate his fortieth birthday on 1 April. Amadu, she revealed to Piers Morgan, was very understanding about their friendship.

'He's very good, because Chris and I are pretty much inseparable and live opposite each other. It's an extraordinary situation that I don't expect anyone else to understand. I said to Amadu when we first started going out that Chris and I had this very special thing and I was never going to give it up, so he would have to accept it. Chris shaped me, made me the way I am. I am so grateful to him.

'Sometimes I get itchy and need to experience some life that isn't just strictly entertainment. It's fantastic, it really is great, but I worked like a crazy person when I was younger and I'm keen to strike more of a balance now. So I'll go to the cinema for an entire day and just do back-to-back movie-watching. And I bought myself this amazing car [a 1989 Porsche 911] that I've wanted since I was a little girl. It's white, with black bumpers and a black leather interior with cream piping. It's so beautiful, I can't believe I'm allowed to drive it – and nor can my dad.'

Life had few downsides, as she explained to *The Works*: 'Sometimes it's a bit of a drag when journalists call you or your family. It would be nicer just to do the job without all that. But over the past five years, I've taken a different approach. Now I get over it. I don't let it become an issue – I just ignore it. It doesn't hurt you that way. I don't read stuff about me any more. If I see a picture of myself in a magazine, I just turn the page. But I still read about everyone else! There's no denying that I love to flick through those celebrity magazines when I'm getting my hair done. I know it's wrong. I recognize that, but once I start reading one of those magazines, I just can't put it down!'

The disappointment of missing out on a BAFTA was tempered when she got to collect one anyway – and then a second – as the BBC emphasized how much she is the real face of *Doctor Who*. The show won Best Drama Series and the Pioneer Audience Award at the Grosvenor House Hotel ceremony in May 2006. David Tennant stepped up to present a third, the Dennis Potter Award for Outstanding TV Writing, to Russell T. Davies.

Immediately wrong-footing the BBC, Billie then announced plans to take a role in an ITV drama, a multi-million-pound adaptation of Jane Austen's *Mansfield Park*, as Fanny Price, the heroine.

There'll be more surprises after that. The next might even be a drama she has penned herself. 'I write a lot,' she said to *The Sunday Times*, 'but I've never actually finished anything I've started. So one day, I hope that I could complete something. I don't know that I want to act for ever and ever – but I always want to be involved with this industry, because I find it exciting and there are lots of different avenues to go down.'

James Nesbitt, her friend and fellow actor, believes Hollywood is inevitable. 'I think she could give the States a crack. I can see her having a career there. But ultimately she'll be Billie Piper.'

America is something for the future. For the time being, Billie is enjoying herself.

'I'm really happy with my life at the moment,' she said. 'I can't imagine things getting better than they are right now.'

Stop Press: As this book was going to the printers, in the middle of June 2006, Billie announced she was quitting *Doctor Who* (again). But this time, Russell T. Davies confirmed the announcement, revealing that Rose Tyler would be written out of the show in the final episode of the second series, to be called 'Doomsday'. It would be, he promised, the scariest *Doctor Who* story ever.

Billie described her two years on the show as 'the most incredible journey' and 'an amazing adventure', but insisted it would come to an end at the climax of series two. The decision had been taken secretly a year earlier and Billie admitted she was scared of leaving. The show made her feel safe … too safe. Her career needed an injection of danger. The gruelling schedule of filming was another factor: she missed Amadu, and wanted to spend time at home with him. On the other hand, she also longed to go backpacking in India and Africa. 'You have to take care of yourself and do what you feel is right,' she said.

And then, leaving the door of the TARDIS open just a little, she added it would be 'an end – for now, at least …'

SOURCES

The author conducted his research using a vast range of sources. These listed were of particular help.

Books

Johnson, Howard, *Ginger Nuts* (Andre Deutsch, 2003)

Magazines

Arena
BBM
Big!
Big Time
Billboard
Bliss
Boyz
FHM
Flipside
GQ
Heat
Hello!
Hit Sensations
J17
Lam
Live & Kicking
Loaded
Looks
Marie Claire
Massive
Maxim
Melody Maker
Ministry
Mizz

Music and Media
My Guy
New Woman
Now
OK!
Q
Radio Times
Red
Select
Shoot
Sky
Smash Hits
Star
Star Girl
STD
Time Out
Top of the Pops
TV Hits
What's On
Woman's Own
The Works
Wow
Zoe

Newspapers

Birmingham Evening Mail
Daily Mail
Daily Record
Daily Star
The Daily Telegraph
Evening News
Evening Post
Evening Standard
Express
The Guardian
Herald and Weekly Times
The Independent

The Independent on Sunday
The Mail on Sunday
Mirror
News of the World
The Observer
Scottish Daily Record
The Sun
Sunday Mirror
Sunday People
The Sunday Times
Swindon Advertiser
The Times

Television

Doctor Who (series one, episode one, 'Rose')
Loose Women
Newsround

Websites

web.archive.org/web/19980710010728/c3.vmg.co.uk/billie/
club/questions/basics.html
archive.thisiswiltshire.co.uk/2001/5/14/218682.html
archive.thisiswiltshire.co.uk/2003/6/17/152773.html
www.bbc.co.uk/pressoffice/pressreleases/stories/2005/
10_october/20/shake_piper.shtml
www.billie-piper.net/id24.html
www.femalefirst.co.uk/entertainment/33972004.htm
www.ideasfactory.com/music_sound/video_profiles/vid_prof
_pop_star.htm
www.myvillage.co.uk/pages/celebs-billiepiper.htm
news.bbc.co.uk/1/hi/entertainment/showbiz/906078.stm
news.bbc.co.uk/1/hi/entertainment/1160393.stm
news.bbc.co.uk/2/hi/uk_news/wales/4858010.stm
www.thestage.co.uk/connect/howto/sylvia.php
www.visimag.com/theworks/a05_feat01.htm
en.wikipedia.org/wiki/Billie_Piper

INDEX